A New Self

A New Self

Self-Therapy with Transactional Analysis

Muriel James and Louis Savary

Addison-Wesley Publishing Company
Reading, Massachusetts • Menlo Park, California
London • Amsterdam • Don Mills, Ontario • Sydney

Library of Congress Cataloging in Publication Data

James, Muriel.
A new self.

Includes bibliographical references.
1.Transactional analysis. 2.Self-perception.
I. Savary, Louis M., joint author. II. Title.
RC489.T7J36 616.8'914 76-55632
ISBN 0-201-03464-6
ISBN 0-201-03463-8 pbk.

Printed in the United States of America. Published simultaneously in Canada. Library of Congress Catalog Card No. 76-55632.

ISBN 0-201-03463-8-P
ISBN 0-201-03464-6-H
ABCDEFGHIJ-DO-7987

Photo credits

Page xiv, Ron Partridge, B.B.M. Associates. Page 2, Ernst Haas, Magnum Photos. Pages 20 and 304, Charles Gatewood, Magnum Photos. Pages 44 and 64, Andy Mercado, Jeroboam. Page 82, Eve Arnold, Magnum Photos. Page 106, Ellis Herwig, Stock, Boston. Page 126, Doug Muir, B.B.M. Associates. Page 142, Jill Freedman, Magnum Photos. Page 158, Rick Smolan, Stock, Boston. Page 176, Leonard Freed, Magnum Photos. Page 194, Burk Uzzle, Magnum Photos. Page 212, Sherry Morgan. Pages 228 and 270, Cary Wolinsky, Stock, Boston. Page 248, Burt Glinn, Magnum Photos. Page 286, H. Cartier-Bresson, Magnum Photos. Page 322, Peter Menzel, Stock, Boston.

Contents

(continued)

PART TWO: THE RELATING SELF

(continued)

Beginning the Adventure

Discovering yourself can be a lifelong adventure. Exploring the ever-unfolding new you can be a fascinating, ever-fresh process of education and therapy.

A New Self is designed to lead you through a process that is both educational and therapeutic. It is educational because it helps you become aware of *what* you need to change. It is therapeutic because it shows you *how* you got to be the way you are and *how* to carry out your program of self-change.

We hope you'll become excited by what you read in these pages and motivated to become involved in the self-discovery process we suggest. Regardless of how you now feel about yourself, you'll begin to feel better *personally* as you work through this book. And, regardless of how poorly or how successfully you now relate to others, you'll begin to make strides *interpersonally* as well. In this process of self-therapy, you'll discover new energies, new potentials, new alternatives, new hope, and ultimately a New Self.

This book is not a substitute for professional psychotherapy. People who have serious emotional problems need to seek professional guidance and should use this book only with their therapists' approval. *A New Self* is for people who are basically mentally healthy, yet want to improve or reorganize themselves in some way.

Most important, *A New Self* can show you how to get in touch with your inner core — that part of self that unifies you — and how to become more aware of your inner urges and energies. In self-therapy, the inner core operates at the deepest personal levels with the urge to live, to love, and to be free. From the inner core come courage and strength, self-affirmation, motivation, and meaning. The inner core is capable of transforming the personality. It is the universal power for self-change, and you can learn how to effectively use it.

All of the exercises in this book have a similar format:

- First, *typical expressions* of people in everyday life set the theme for the activity and suggest how others have dealt with that theme.
- Next, *theoretical statements* summarize a particular idea in the self-therapy process.

- And finally, *personalized activities,* based on the theory, help you create, step by step, a New Self.

Although some people may not need to work through the entire book, we encourage everyone, for the sake of completeness, to do most of the exercises — especially those toward which you feel some resistance or ambivalence.

People who have worked through *A New Self* report that it is a potent tool for self-change. They have also said they would like to repeat many of the exercises annually to see how they have changed and grown. For this reason, you may want to use a notebook for your answers instead of writing them directly in the book. In this way, you can again assess your personal growth without being influenced by last year's answers.

Transactional Analysis, often called TA for short, is a widely practiced and highly effective approach to self-change. Its creator, psychiatrist Dr. Eric Berne, introduced TA with his best-seller, *Games People Play.* Thomas Harris's *I'm OK, You're OK* and Muriel James and Dorothy Jongeward's *Born to Win* further popularized TA theory. Without relying on jargon or technical language, TA helps people better understand themselves and others. We feel that it is both an enjoyable and practical approach to self-discovery and self-improvement, so we've structured *A New Self* around TA ideas and processes. This book includes many of the new TA theories and techniques that have been developed since *Games People Play* and *Born to Win.*

We've divided the book into two parts. With Part I, you can learn to understand and create a *new individual self;* with Part II, you can learn how to understand and create a *new relating self* and a third, *transpersonal self.* Hundreds of new exercises are included that you can use to:

- Make effective contracts for individual growth and for learning to relate to others.
- Change or enhance your life plan, or "psychological script."

- Think more clearly and express ideas more clearly through re-Adulting.
- Be a better parent to your children, to other people, or even to yourself through re-Parenting.
- Overcome negative influences in your childhood and recover a sense of joy through re-Childing.
- Recognize negative psychological games and give them up in favor of openness and authenticity.
- Analyze the ways you spend time with others and learn how to use your time creatively.

Although a few activities in this book may seem familiar, most will be unfamiliar, some even unusual. But they work. We know. We've successfully tried them on ourselves, our friends, our students, and our clients, and we now want to share them with anyone who is interested in becoming a New Self.

Muriel James
Lafayette, California

Louis Savary
South Belmar, New Jersey

March 1977

Part One

The Individual Self

1 The Challenge of Change

The sense of self

Most people are interested in understanding themselves and say so with such phrases as: "I wish I knew myself better"; or, "I really want to understand myself"; or, "I wish I could control myself"; or, "I wish I were more in touch with myself."

The deepest part of the self is traditionally described by words such as heart, soul, spirit, spiritual core, essence, substance, and so forth. Some simply add an adjective to the word "self" and describe this inner essence as the "real self," the "undivided self," the "integrated self," the "transpersonal self," or the "fully human self."

These expressions point to the belief that the self is, paradoxically, both uniquely personal and universally human.

People reveal the importance they attach to their *unique* human qualities in expressions such as, "I can't stand myself," or "I like myself." The importance they attach to their *universal* human qualities is similarly revealed in statements such as, "I wish I could feel more in touch with humanity," or "Now that I've got myself together, I feel like part of the human race." By these statements, people verbalize their like or dislike for some part of themselves.

What we mean by "self" is the you that is both uniquely personal and universally human. Everyone experiences their self in these two ways: as having a *unique* historical identity, and as having a *shared* identity by being part of the human race.

Furthermore, the self can be continually fresh and new. A three-year-old child expressed it well. "Grandma," he said, "People are so *new* when they're born and I'm *still* new." He then looked up thoughtfully at her and added, "And so are you." She is his unique, unforgettable Grandma, yet she is a "new" person, changing all the time.

The power to change

Some people don't like themselves and want to change. Others do like themselves, yet also want to change in certain ways. Both want to let go of some parts of their old self in order to develop a more lively, more competent, more loving new self. To change is a challenge.

In one sense, to develop an entirely new self is impossible. You will never cease to be the "self that is you" and you will always reflect some of your past programming and conditioning. In another sense, a new self *is* possible, because the "self that is you" is an ever-unfolding adventure of self-actualization.

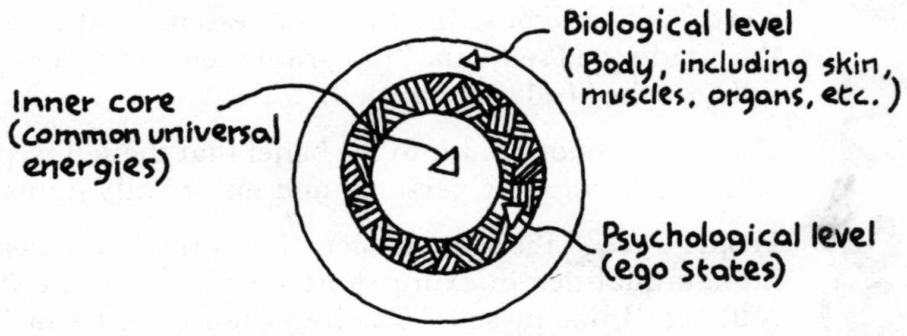

Self experienced on three levels: biological, psychological, inner core

With each new actualizing moment, the "self that is you" is experienced in different ways. It is experienced (1) in your inner core; (2) through your unique personality, which shows through your ego states; and (3) through your body, which lives on this planet in this period of time, expressing itself in movements, feeling, words, gestures, body warmth, and sensory response. Though you are "unchangeably" the person you were, say, ten years ago, you may still honestly describe yourself today as a "new" person, changing all the time.

People may deliberately create a new self by using energy generated from their "urge to live" — an urge all healthy selves experience in their inner core. This urge is expressed as: the urge to be a free person; the urge to relate to others; the urge to have experiences and to understand them; and the urge to make decisions.

Often these universal urges and energies go unexplored because people do not realize they have them, or do not know how to use them, or have allowed these energies to fall into disuse or neglect. Each of these specific inner-core energies needs to be employed in creating a new self.

The *urge to be free* releases energies to grow, to break through archaic ways of thinking and behaving, and to create new patterns in the *personal* self.

The *urge to relate* releases energies for seeking out other people, for working or playing with them in cooperation and intimacy. This urge is crucial in creating a new *relating* self.

The *urge to experience new things* and to analyze the experiences releases energies for exploring both inner and outer worlds, subjectively and objectively. Your own ability to experience yourself both subjectively through feelings and objectively through analytical thought will be most helpful to you in self-therapy, that is, in shaping a new self.

The *urge to make decisions* releases energies to make agreements and to carry them out. During a process of self-change, you will learn how to activate these essential energies in meaningful ways.

The basic urge to live, expressed in these energies, gives people the power to change.

Ingredients for self-change

Any program for a new self is based on the belief that people possess the freedom-energy to change some things about themselves and their world.

Most people realize that if they want to improve themselves, they need to change. Sometimes change is easy, sometimes it is not.

For example, many people often refer to their habits as things they "can't change." It is easier to stay in a rut than to struggle at getting out. When unhealthy ways of thinking and acting become ingrained, change requires *courage*. This quality stems from the self's capacity to make a decision.

Effective change also requires *motivation*. Many people would willingly adopt a new way of thinking and acting if they could find a reason for it. The ability to find a reason, to find meanings, stems from the self's capacity to evaluate situations objectively.

But even when people are motivated and courageous enough to change, they sometimes fail in their attempt. Frequently, the missing ingredient is their lack of information, their lack of a plan — a practical program for change. The changes they hope for are vague and unrealistic, "pie in the sky" fantasies that are not related to the here and now. Effective change calls for realistic *planning*.

These three ingredients — courage, motivation, and planning — are needed for a successful program of self-therapy to develop a new self.

The courage to change

Many people, after an unsuccessful attempt to change or improve themselves, grow discouraged, even despairing. The courage needed for self-change is not the opposite of discouragement or despair but, as Rollo May describes in *The Courage to Create*, "Courage is, rather, the capacity to move ahead *in spite of despair.*" Courage calls upon energy, or strength, from the inner core that underlies all we say, feel, think, and do. Courage urges people on despite failure, discouragement, or despair.

Thus, the opposite of courage is not despair, but *apathy*, the inability to make a personal encounter or a commitment. A courageous decision to change, when change is necessary, leads to a commitment, a total personal involvement.

Courage has the same root as the French word *coeur*, which means heart. Courage operates from the "heart," or center of who we are, and directs us toward self-actualization. It enables us to make commitments. The inner core pours this energy for commitment through our selves in much the same way that our hearts pump blood through our bodies. As stated by James and Jongeward in *Born to Win:*

> It takes courage to accept intimacy and directly encounter other persons, courage to take a stand in an unpopular cause, courage to choose authenticity over approval and to choose it again and again, courage to accept the responsibility for your own choices, and, indeed, courage to be the very unique person you really are.[1]

Motivation and meaning

To carry out a program of self-change, people need not only courage and commitment, they also need motivation. Sick people may visit physicians because they are motivated to get well. Hungry people may stop at a restaurant because they are motivated to eat. Unhappy people may visit psychotherapists because they are motivated to regain mental health. Uninformed people may go to school because they are motivated to learn more. In each case, the motivation may be traced to the inner core and its energies, urging the self towards meaningful change.

People want to change and improve themselves for a variety of reasons. The stronger their motivation, the likelier they are to reach their desired change. According to Viktor E. Frankl, a search for meaning is one of the strongest human motivations. He reports that many people are motivated more deeply by a "search for meaning" than by a "search for self."

The continuing search for meaning provides ever richer sources of motivation for self-actualization, both for people with already healthy selves and for those whose selves are not so healthy.

Many healthy people are attracted to self-therapy. They are motivated to "get better," "be happier," "be more free"; their decision for self-change is motivated by a desire to carry out their meaning and purpose in life, and to do it more effectively.

Other people are not so healthy. Some of them believe that life has little or no meaning and say such things as, "There's no meaning, no reason to go on." They tend to despair. Others fight desperately for "self" survival, like drowning persons struggling to keep afloat. Others slowly give up. Each of these not-so-healthy people needs to develop the meanings in life they already have and to discover new ones. In their search for meaning, they learn to overcome obstacles that interfere with their self-actualization. The important question, of course, is: How does one do all this?

The business of self-actualization, according to Abraham H. Maslow, can best be carried out "via a commitment to an important job." Maslow's suggestion offers a significant way to personal growth, once people can identify their important "jobs."

Many activities, such as raising a family, caring for a sick person, traveling abroad, going to college, or keeping a garden, are important jobs, for they make sense to the people doing them and add meaning to their lives. The scientist's search for truth and the artist's search for beauty can also be meaningful tasks. So, too, the struggle to be more loving, to be more authentic with others, and to respond with empathy to suffering.

Self-therapy itself can also be an important and meaningful job. It can become a personal encounter with truth and beauty. It may also involve suffering. It certainly requires motivation in overcoming resistance to change.

Since the process of self-therapy requires motivation for its completion, it usually develops into a search for meaning. *The search for meaning is a primary motivating force in each human life.*

Each person's meanings are unique and specific. Your meanings are personal to you; they can only be discovered and realized by you.

As people discover the many personal meanings they have, their inner-core energies are being tapped and released. In these energies, they discover the courage to fulfill their meanings. People who find meaning in their life and work feel strengthened physically and psychologically. Vitally alive, they energetically pursue other significant meanings, more fully and freely than before.

Planning for change

Changing yourself for the better takes planning. It almost never happens by accident. Behind every successful self-change, especially those intended to enrich life's meaning, lies a realistic plan.

Changing yourself is a process with many stages. Usually change begins with a vague idea, a wish, a need, a dream, a fantasy, or a suggestion that slowly begins to clarify itself. For example, someone might say, "I wish I could see myself feeling comfortable and acting friendly in a new social situation, even making friends." The self-change process may stop at this point, or it may move on to a second stage.

This next stage involves making plans. People sense that they are capable of improving themselves, and realize that their dream needs to be translated into a concrete plan if it is to become a reality.

Step-by-step planning involves having a clear idea of what is wanted, a plan for getting it, and a way of evaluating progress. Some plans do not initially produce the desired results. Therefore, plans need to be evaluated and revised frequently.

To carry out the plan, materials and tools are needed. In self-therapy the materials are you — your personal history, goals and talents, the way you use your feelings and intellect, as well as how you use your capacities and limitations. Some tools for self-therapy may be found in this book. You will need to use both materials *and* tools to implement your plan.

Implementing means putting a plan into action; this involves doing the necessary work and evaluating the results. Implementing takes time as well as courage and motivation. However, in the end you have found new meaning for your life and created a more lively, loving, and lovable new self.

Creativity for a new self

Creativity is the act of bringing something new into being.

Self-therapy, as a form of self-creativity, is not meant to be an experience of *trying*, but to be an experience of *trusting*. Trusting the self-therapy process leads to absorption in the project and to giving it a high priority. Like an artist committed to creating a piece of art, people in self-therapy need to give *themselves* priority. They need to be intensely involved in the creative act of bringing a new self into being. They need to trust themselves and the powers of their inner core to work together for their own good.

When people are totally absorbed in a task, the energy needed for its completion is present. They discover new excitement, new meanings, new "whys" to live for.

"Life is just one meaningless event after another."

"I'd be willing to die for my spouse and children."

People often disagree on whether or not life has meaning. Some think it has great meaning. Because life "makes sense" to them, it therefore has meaning. Others suffer from a sort of inner emptiness and can find no meaning worth living for. Some give up; others search to discover a *why* to motivate their lives.

Do you believe that a person needs something or someone to live for? ________ Why do you think that? ____________

Is there something or someone in your life that you live for? ________ If so, who and why? ____________________

Is there something or someone in your life that you would die for if necessary? ________ If yes, why is that so? ________

____

What are some different things that have meaning for other people? ____________________________________

What are some things they might live for? ____________

What might they die for? ________________________

____

11 *Meanings found in tasks*

"I find meaning in raising a family."

"For me, it's my job."

"Working for social change is important to me."

People find meaning — that which makes sense to them — in many ways. According to Viktor Frankl, these ways are expressed in three basic patterns:

- In creatively *achieving a task* — planning it, working on it, completing it.
- In *positive experiences* of love, truth, beauty, or of knowing one or more persons deeply in all their uniqueness.
- In *coping with one's own or other people's suffering when it cannot be avoided.*[2]

List some tasks you have done or observed other people doing that didn't seem to make sense because they lacked meaning. Do the same for tasks that have had meaning. Explain why each of these tasks was with or without meaning.

Tasks with little or no meaning	*No meaning because*
____________________	____________________
____________________	____________________

Tasks with much meaning	*Have meaning because*
____________________	____________________
____________________	____________________

If your life is full of meaningless tasks, you either need to find value and meaning in them or change yourself or your tasks in some way.

"Seeing the first spring blossoms popping open gives the winter some meaning."

"Loving and being loved by my family is the most meaningful thing in my life."

"The never-ending search for truth is important to me."

From time to time, everyone enjoys positive experiences of love, truth, and beauty. These moments of beauty or relationships of love transcend everyday experiences and add meaning to life. Abraham Maslow calls these high points "peak experiences," and suggests that self-actualizing people enjoy them often and in different spheres of life. Yet each peak experience is unique. Each is related to a concrete situation of love, truth, unity, beauty, or joy and laughter.

List some of the big and little positive experiences of love, truth, unity, beauty, or joy and laughter that have given your life meaning. Select transcending experiences that are not directly related to your work, accomplishments, or tasks.

Transcending experiences I have known	*Who or what was actually involved?*	*What meaning did the event have?*

"If I hadn't given her one of my kidneys, she would have died."

"Taking care of my mother in her final months gave our relationship new meaning."

"When I hurt I can hardly stand it, yet I want to keep going for the sake of my kids."

To suffer physically from hunger or thirst or from humid heat or incapacitating cold is always painful, sometimes even fatal. Also painful are physical handicaps, accidents, illnesses, or operations people endure or experience. If physical suffering can be avoided, it should be. If it cannot be avoided, and for most people the day ultimately comes when it cannot, then the search for meaning related to unavoidable suffering is crucial for the courageous person.

Jot down how you have known physical suffering personally, how you have experienced it with other people you know, or how you have observed it on the stage or on television. How was it dealt with? With courage or nobility? With stoicism or denial? Cowardice or whining? Tears or anger? What meaning may have been found in the suffering?

Experiences of suffering	*Responses to the suffering*	*Possible meanings found*
____________	____________	____________
____________	____________	____________
____________	____________	____________

"I'll need my sense of humor wherever I go."

"My politeness has always helped me."

"My mind is my best ally."

"Since childhood, I've tried to be honest with myself."

One of the most important steps in learning how to change or improve involves deciding what to keep. People's personal meanings and purposes in life influence what personal qualities they choose to keep. Self-therapy helps people assess themselves and their strengths in order to build on them. In developing a new self, no one needs to get totally rid of what they have been and currently are.

Make a list of some of your strengths and values that you find meaningful and would like to keep and build on.

Strengths I have and like	*Potential strengths I need to develop*
____________________	____________________
____________________	____________________
____________________	____________________
____________________	____________________
____________________	____________________
____________________	____________________
____________________	____________________
____________________	____________________

"I could do better without my foul tongue."

"I'd be better off if I stopped procrastinating."

"I'd like to drop a few pounds."

"I wish I weren't so shy."

"I have a nice way with people, but I don't use it enough."

Besides deciding which personal qualities to keep, it's important also to decide which to let go. The wish to let go of a personal inadequacy indicates that it probably has little meaning or value for you at present, or that it serves no purpose in its present form.

Self-therapy asks people to become aware of those personality weaknesses that need to be changed and ways of behaving that need to be discarded.

List those things about you that you would like to be rid of, or would like to have changed in some way.

Things I want to let go of	*How to start letting go*
______________________	______________________
______________________	______________________
______________________	______________________
______________________	______________________
______________________	______________________
______________________	______________________
______________________	______________________

"Whenever I feel pressured, I lose my courage."

"I want to change; I guess it's up to me to do it."

"Sometimes when I'm scared, I have to force myself."

Most people need courage — not necessarily for combat, but simply for the struggles of daily life, for making it through a tough day. They need courage to live life to the fullest, and to live life fully often requires self-change. Since facing a need to change may be difficult, it helps if people get in touch with the beliefs they have about their own courage to change. It also helps to be aware of previous situations where courage was needed.

Recall some situations in your life when you faced a challenge to change yourself, when you needed courage and may have felt inadequate to the challenge. How did it work out?

Situations that required courage (where I felt very inadequate, scared, or panicked)	*What I did about the situation and about my feelings*	*Was what I did courageous or not?*

"When my husband suddenly died, I had to take over."

"My kids say I'm boring and won't be seen with me."

"If I had more skills, I could get a job."

"I'd rather be excited than just lukewarm."

Crisis and boredom are two experiences that commonly motivate people to examine their lives and their values. Crisis always shocks. Death, illness, and accidents are some of the more obvious traumatic events. Yet being uprooted from home or job can also bring about a crisis; so, too, can the departure of a close friend or neighbor. Whether the crisis seems large or small, those involved feel a sense of shock. They may respond courageously or they may not.

Boredom, a devastating experience, also motivates people to change — to change themselves, their jobs, their friends, their use of leisure time, and so on. Underneath the bored feeling often lies a feeling of resentment. Such resentment is usually directed against others who do not make life more exciting for the bored person.

Complete the following lists to get in touch with the motivations for change that you have experienced.

Crisis events or feelings of boredom that motivated me to change	*Related changes I have made*	*New meanings the changes gave my life*
______________	______________	______________
______________	______________	______________
______________	______________	______________
______________	______________	______________

"No one ever taught me how to *plan*."

"My parents simply commanded me to change, they never showed me how."

"The only approach I know is trial-and-error."

"I don't know where to begin."

"Change just happens, doesn't it?"

Some people seldom plan. They tend to do things on the spur of the moment. Others make inadequate, inappropriate, or grandiose plans.

The skill of planning is often related to past experiences and the amount of accurate information that is available. People can learn by their experiences and plan better when they have a second chance. So, too, do they plan better when they have objective facts to work from.

Fill in the following: As a planner, I see myself as

________________ (adequate, inadequate). The kinds of plans I make are often

_________. I think this is because I ___________. Generally

speaking, I _________ (am, am not) satisfied with my planning abilities.

What I might want to improve about my planning is

___________. This would enhance my new self because I

would then ___________.

"When I die, I want to leave the world a better place."

"I've always helped others. That's important for me."

"Laughing and playing with others means the most to me."

"The meaning of my life is just to endure one day at a time."

People who see their lives as having meaning can integrate their past experiences, live in the present, and look forward toward the future.

Perhaps your past, present and future can be synthesized into a single statement that describes your basic philosophy, your meaning and purpose in life. Such a statement may clarify your direction for self-change and energize the entire self-therapy process.

Complete the following:

From the personal reflection I've done in this chapter so far, the central meaning or purpose in my life might be summarized in the words: ______________________

____

Or, if someone asked me, "What is the meaning of your life now?" I might respond: ______________________

____

Personality Plus

Your self is your uniqueness, that which makes you *you*. Being alive grants you the freedom to change yourself, to be objective, to deliberate, and to decide how to change. These capacities are limited by the fact that you are also finite — living in your body, on this earth, at this particular time in history — and you may need help in understanding yourself and the people with whom you live and work.

Transactional Analysis, the psychological basis of this book, offers both a *theory* and a *method* to achieve this personal and interpersonal insight. By exploring how TA works, you can learn to apply its principles in shaping your new self.

The power of imagination

Learning how to use TA involves imagination, a capacity that at times can prove misleading. A child observing a parent's frown may, for example, mistakenly *imagine* the parent is angry, when actually the parent is merely deep in thought. Parents may mistakenly *imagine* their teenage children are "up to no good" when they stay out late; actually, the teens are merely talking with each other at a friend's home. In this book, we hope to show you ways to use your imagination accurately.

Imagination is a potent capacity. People use it often, especially when daydreaming. Sometimes they can transform their daydreams into plans and their plans into realities; sometimes they recognize the impossibility of realizing their imaginative plans. In planning your self-change, you will discover you can depend significantly on your imaginative power.

However, there are some people who use their powerful imaginative capacities in destructive ways. They negatively imagine themselves to be what they aren't instead of positively imagining themselves to be what they want to be. For example, people who think of themselves as ugly often appear ugly to others as well — their poor self-concept communicates a negative visual image. In contrast, people who picture themselves as beautiful often shine with an inner confidence and actually appear beautiful to others. Using imagination positively in the context of TA, people learn to see themselves realistically, learn to think in constructive ways, and learn how to become a new self.

When people imagine themselves to be courageous, highly motivated, and able to plan, these qualities are reflected in their actions. The reverse is also true. Losers imagine themselves as losers and become that way. Winners imagine themselves as winners and act so that they are.[1] Imagination's capacity to affect people's lives in dramatic ways needs to be taken into account in any self-change program.

The understanding imagination

Imagination may also be used to clarify ideas, to picture abstract concepts, to enrich experience, and to promote understanding.

In initially exploring TA, people are asked to imagine (later they will discover it is true) that within each individual person are three ego states, called Parent, Adult, and Child. These ego states are consistent patterns of feeling and experience related to consistent patterns of behavior.

When you are thinking, feeling, and acting as your parents once did, you are in your Parent ego state. When you are thinking, feeling, and acting as you did in childhood, you are in your Child ego state. And, when you are thinking, feeling, and acting as a rational, realistic, objective, data-processing person, you are in your Adult ego state. When the words Parent, Adult, or Child are capitalized in this book, they refer to ego states; when not, they refer to people.

Eric Berne, originator of TA, diagrammed the human personality as shown in the accompanying ego state diagrams. The line enclosing the three ego states represents the body layer of the person, which is the outer container of the inner personality.

Everyone's personality contains these three ego states. Even young children have an Adult ego state with which they are able to think and act rationally. Understanding how and when these ego states are used is one of the first steps in deciding what needs to be changed to create a new self.

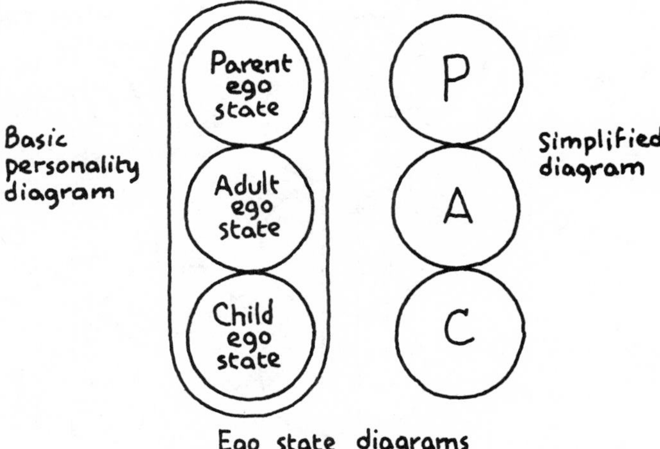

Ego state diagrams

The plus of personality

The plus part of personality is called the *inner core.* It refers to the deepest self, an individual's permanent identity, the source of personal strength, energy, and meaning. It can be healthy and generate life in each of the ego states, much like a healthy apple core stimulates the growth of an apple. Or it can be closed off and repressed so that the ego states cannot act in healthy ways. If the latter is true, the diseased inner core may generate the illness, atrophy, and death of the whole. Statements such as, "I'm sick at heart" or "He's rotten to the core" or "I feel good all the way through" or "I'm at peace in the center of my being," are verbal expressions of inner-core feelings.

The inner core, the *plus* part of personality, can also be diagrammed (p.24). The left figure shows when the inner core is closed off and its energy cannot flow into the ego states. The right figure illustrates an open inner core where courage and motivation flow freely through the ego states. Such an open, energized person usually finds meaning in much of life.

This chapter focuses on the ego states and how to analyze them; it also introduces you to the inner core. Further discussion of the inner core and how to release its power can be found in Chapter 10.

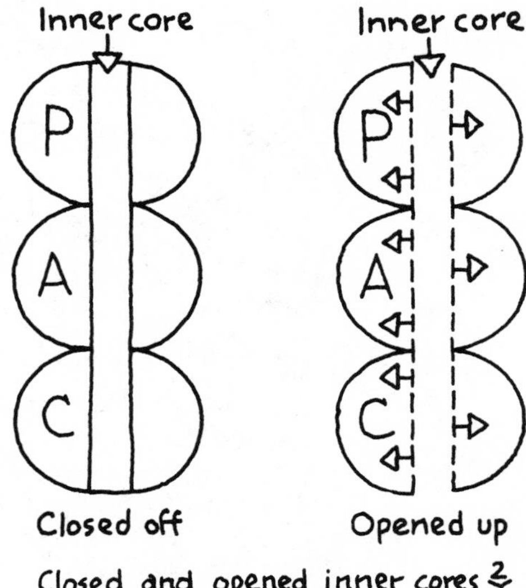

Closed and opened inner cores[2]

Eric Berne, the originator of TA, hinted at what we are calling the inner core. He used the term "real Self" to describe it.

> This real person is probably the real Self, the one which can move from one ego state to another. When people get to know each other well, they penetrate through the script *into the depths where this real Self resides,* and that is the part of the other person they respect and love, and with which they can have moments of real intimacy. . . .[3]

A "new self" develops because of changes made in the ego states *through the power that can be released from the inner core.* Eric Berne, in describing what he calls Self's activity, says, "It is like a charge of electricity that is free to jump from one capacitor to another, regardless of what the capacitors are used for."[4] For us, this power or charge comes from the inner core. It is capable of transforming the personality; it is the power for self-change.

Originally, Transactional Analysis theory did not include the concept of the inner core. This concept was developed by Muriel James in her book *Born to Love* and introduced again in our book *The Power at the Bottom of the Well.* As co-authors, we are stressing the importance of a person's inner core in self-therapy because it operates at the deepest personal levels with the urges to live, to love, and to be free. From the inner core comes courage and strength, self-affirmation, motivation, and meaning.

"You act just like your mother."

"Aren't you ever going to grow up?"

"I like the way you think."

"Sometimes I feel like a big baby."

"It's fun figuring out new things."

"In many ways, I'm the image of my father."

When people are in the Adult ego state, they act rationally, think clearly, function on the basis of facts, and exchange information with others. In the Parent ego state, they act as their parent figures once acted and adopt their opinions and ways of doing things. In the Child ego state, they feel and act as they did in childhood.

List two things you did or said recently that were well thought out and based on factual information.

____

____

List two things you did or said recently that were similar to what one of your parent figures once did or said.

____

____

List two things you did, said, or felt recently that resembled your childhood behavior.

____

____

"Wow, I feel good!"

"I often feel so stupid and inadequate."

"Gee, it's just what I wanted!"

"I'm always scared in new situations."

"No matter how hard I try, I can't make it."

The Child ego state is that part of the personality that is like an actual child. Each person's childhood is unique; therefore, each person's Child ego state differs somewhat from everyone else's. The Child functions in three basic ways. The adapted Child initiates situations and responds to situations on the basis of early training and traumas. The naturally free Child is creative, impulsive, and intuitive in initiating situations, and responds on the basis of wanting pleasure and wanting to avoid pain.

Answer the questions that follow to recognize how your Child ego state commonly expresses itself.

	That's me	*That's not me*
I was trained not to show my feelings.	( )	( )
I constantly try to please people.	( )	( )
I often feel like getting even.	( )	( )
I'm frequently depressed (confused, angry, sad, scared, etc.).	( )	( )
I feel happy a lot.	( )	( )
I was never allowed to decide for myself. I still have trouble making up my mind.	( )	( )

"I'll need more facts before deciding."

"It's too expensive for my budget this month."

"How can this be fixed?"

The Adult is the rational, logical, reasonable, reflective part of the personality. It operates by thinking and collecting data from inner and outer experience. It processes facts and information, and evaluates what it learns.

While doing the exercises in this book, you are almost always using your Adult ego state. Even when you are asked to describe your Child feelings or locate a Parent value, it is your Adult at work gathering this information and organizing it.

Think of a recent decision you made and examine how your Parent, Adult, and Child ego states influenced your decision.

	That's me	*That's not me*
Parent ego state influence		
Did you decide as one of your parents would have?	( )	( )
Child ego state influence		
Did you decide on the basis of your feelings?	( )	( )
Adult ego state influence		
Did you have all the facts needed?	( )	( )
Did you ignore some important facts?	( )	( )
Did you find evidence to show that your decision was the best one for you?	( )	( )

"You should know better!"

"Here, let me help you, you'll never do it."

"You can't trust those kinds of people."

People, when in their Parent ego state, often use words like "should," "ought," "must," "always," "never." The Parent ego state expresses itself in punitive and controlling ways or in caring and nurturing ways. As a controlling Parent, a person's statements may take the form of absolute rules, commands, and orders. As a nurturing Parent, statements may express care and concern.

When people are in their Parent ego states, they may motivate others by offering rewards or threatening punishment. They do this in unique ways copied from their own parents.

Make lists of things your parents said or did that you liked or disliked when you were little. Also list some things for which you were rewarded and others for which you were punished.

Things I liked	*Things I disliked*
______________________	______________________
______________________	______________________

Things rewarded	*Things punished*
______________________	______________________
______________________	______________________

Now, put a check beside each behavior your parents used that you sometimes use.

"That might mean something to my father, but not to me."

"I feel stale unless I'm using my brains."

Even as the whole self seeks its personal meaning and purpose, each ego state also seeks its own special meanings. For example, the Parent seems to find its strongest meaning in customs, traditions, and rules; the Adult looks for meaning primarily in reasoning and decision making; the Child seems to seek its meaning in experiences and feelings of pleasure and pain. When life in general, or a situation in particular, seems meaningless, it may be because one or more of the ego states resists or dislikes the situation, instead of being attracted to it or cooperating with it.

The *universal* self, the inner core with its urge to deliberate and decide, continually searches for meanings that will help deal with the pressures that arise from external sources or from internal ego states.

Look back at the exercises in Chapter 1, at the meanings you have found in specific tasks, in positive experiences, and in unavoidable suffering. List them next to the ego state with which they seem to be most closely associated.

	Specific tasks	Positive experiences	Unavoidable Suffering
P	________	________	________
	________	________	________
A	________	________	________
	________	________	________
C	________	________	________
	________	________	________

"When things go wrong, I freeze up and can't think or move."

"I'm often up then down, up then down, just like a yo-yo."

"In a crisis, I can really make good decisions."

Most people experience ego-state boundaries as semipermeable. They can feel energy flow from the inner core into their ego states and from one ego state to another. Sometimes energy flows slowly, sometimes quickly.

For example, soft music may elicit an *easy* flow of energy from the thinking Adult to the pleasure-seeking Child. In contrast a sudden loud noise may elicit a *rush* of energy to an ego state. Some people might interpret a loud noise as a fearful catastrophe, so in them the energy rushes to the Child. Others hearing the same loud noise might mobilize their Adult energy to find out where the noise comes from and what it means. Still others might activate their Parent energy and be critical of the noise, or perhaps concerned about how the noise is disturbing others.

Imagine the following situations and respond as quickly as possible, giving your intuition free play.

If the house caught on fire,

my Parent might ______________________

my Adult might ______________________

my Child might ______________________

If I suddenly won $10,000 on a sweepstakes ticket,

my Parent might ____________________

my Adult might ____________________

my Child might ____________________

If somebody I consider important criticized me,

my Parent might ____________________

my Adult might ____________________

my Child might ____________________

If I saw a small child being severely spanked in a grocery store,

my Parent might ____________________

my Adult might ____________________

my Child might ____________________

If I was offered a new job that would necessitate my moving away from family and friends,

my Parent might ____________________

my Adult might ____________________

my Child might ____________________

Generally speaking, my ________ ego state seems strongest in the above fantasized situations.

"He's always so analytical!"

"She's continually putting others down."

"I can't seem to control my temper."

People learn during childhood how to act in order to survive. Some discover that to survive they have to act like a parent to others in the family. Some discover they can get what they want with temper tantrums, tears, or sulkiness. Still others are encouraged to think for themselves and be self-sufficient. Although most people do all of these things at one time or another, many people have a "favorite" ego state that they use more often than others.

Consider the last twenty-four hours. Estimate how much time you spent in each ego state:

		Hours or minutes
P	Directing or advising others	______
	Taking care of others	______
A	Thinking analytically	______
	Acting rationally	______
C	Acting like an obedient child	______
	Acting like a rebellious child	______
	Acting like a playful child	______

33 *Blocked energy*

"Some days I just can't think."

"Some days I seem to block off all my feelings."

"Some days I wish I didn't have children — I'm tired of always being Mom."

Many people use certain of their ego states more frequently than others. People who *continually* use the same ego state may experience an energy blockage to the other two ego states — inner energy can't seem to penetrate into these unused spheres. It's as if their ego state boundaries are no longer permeable, but have become calcified and rigid instead.

People with energy blocks may continually express the adaptations and feelings from their Child, or continually think as a mechanistic computing Adult, or continually advise or take care of others from their Parent. They need to relax their rigid ego boundaries so that energy can flow freely. Until boundaries are permeable, such people may not feel courageous, motivated, or able to plan.

Watch popular figures on television and note those that continually use one or two ego states and deny expression of others.

Name	*How their ego states show*
____________________	______________________________________
____________________	______________________________________

Now get comfortable, close your eyes and look at yourself as though looking at TV. Do you naturally use all three of your ego states? Do you see yourself as blocking off any of your energy? If so, how?

____

"Whenever I want to have some fun, I recall my father saying, 'Work before pleasure'."

" 'You can do it,' my mom used to say, and I know I can."

"Whenever I feel bad I hear the motto, 'Don't cry over spilt milk,' so I don't show my feelings."

Knowingly or unknowingly, people talk to themselves. They often have an inner argument, usually between the Parent and Child ego states, on what they should or shouldn't do. The inner Child, says Eric Berne, is somewhat like a ventriloquist's dummy responding to the inner Parent either with compliance or with rebellion.

Recall a recent encounter with someone. What did you say to yourself after it was over? ______________________________

____

Remember a recent mistake you made. What was the inner dialogue after you discovered it? ____________________

____

Think of a future event you have scheduled. Which ego states in you say what to you? ______________________________

____

"I won't hire someone like that. Those people are all lazy."

"Sex is only for procreation, and don't forget it!"

"On public transportation you should always give your seat to a woman."

"Women don't become doctors, they become nurses."

❧

The Adult's clear-thinking capacity is often contaminated by opinions and prejudices from the Parent ego state. People are seldom aware of prejudices and biases operating within themselves. They often think they are rationally Adult when, as a matter of fact, their thinking is contaminated and influenced by their Parent rules, opinions, and attitudes. A contaminated Adult results in foggy thinking. It is diagrammed as:

Adult ego state contaminated by Parent opinions

Parental contamination of the Adult ego state may be expressed in prejudices against people of a different race, religion, education, vocation, etc. It may also be expressed in inflexible lifestyles and traditions. In extreme cases, people experience Parental contaminations as hallucinations which may totally block out the Adult.

❧

(continued)

Quickly write the adjectives or phrases that you commonly apply to the following groups of people.

Men are:	*Women are:*
______________________	______________________
______________________	______________________
______________________	______________________

Children should be:	*Everyone should be:*
______________________	______________________
______________________	______________________
______________________	______________________

Now study your lists. Where you do not have substantial and *objective* facts to support your responses, your thinking may have been fogged up by your Parent ego state.

"I sometimes sound confused when speaking."

"I often think I'm right, then find out I'm not."

"I tend to let my feelings rule my actions."

"I've been told that I'm always changing my mind."

When the Child contaminates the Adult, delusions, illusions, and wishful childlike feelings interfere with clear, direct thinking. This happens because children learn to think unrealistically about themselves and others. Child contamination is diagrammed as:

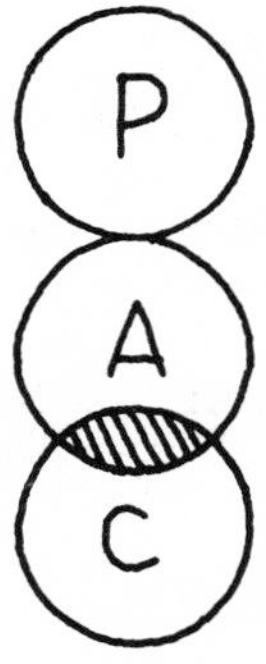

Adult ego state contaminated by Child feelings and adaptations

For example, a little girl who learns to think of herself as stupid when she really isn't has a hard time later on realistically assessing her actual intelligence. A little boy who learns to think he's not a real boy because he's small and not good at football may have a hard time as a grownup accepting that he's an OK male.

Some people keep their childhood illusions. Most of us, for example, believe in some form of magic. That is, we may believe *things* will bring us happiness or we may believe that if we *try* hard enough, or *wait* long enough, something magical will happen.[5]

(continued)

Contaminations ebb and flow. People are contaminated in different ways and different situations. The most common Child contamination occurs when feelings interfere with thinking.

Write down a recent situation in which you *imagined* you had to live up to someone's expectations.

What *feelings* did you experience?

How did your feelings affect you?

"I'm 40 years old and still being bossed by my parents."

"I fall apart when things go wrong."

"Everyone tells me their problems. I get tired of it."

"I like to think before I act."

Ego states are activated in many ways. An unexpected comment, event, or problem may stimulate, for example, strong feelings of helplessness (like a child) or of helpfulness (like a nurturing parent) or of thoughtfulness (like a rational adult). Learning how to analyze your ego states when you solve problems is an important process in designing a new self.[6]

Select a problem you would like to solve. Describe it briefly.

The problem is ______________________________

Mom would say ____ | MOM | DAD | Dad would say ______

and do ______________ | | | and do ______________

and feel ____________ | | | and feel ____________

Facts I already have: | A | Facts I need to get:

______________________ | | ______________________

______________________ | | ______________________

My basic uncensored feelings about this are: ____________ | C | The feelings I learned to have about things like this are: ________

My hunch is: ______________________________

"I'm going to stop being so critical."

"I'll make sounder decisions if I get more facts."

"I'm going to take better care of my body."

"I can think when I put my mind to it."

Contracts are agreements people make with themselves and with others. Contracts that succeed are those that the Adult makes, that the Child is willing to go along with, and that the Parent will not overrule too strenuously. In subsequent chapters you will be structuring a new self through techniques of self re-Childing, re-Parenting, and Re-Adulting. This exercise is a preview of what you can do with self-contracts.

Think about yourself and the "ideal self" you want to be. Then, think of adjectives that describe these ego states.

	My ego states now		*The way I want them to be*	
Parent	_______	_______	_______	_______
Adult	_______	_______	_______	_______
Child	_______	_______	_______	_______

Now consider what you would need to do differently to make the adjectives you wish for actually apply to you.

____

____

____

____

"Sometimes I really experience something from the center of my being."

"No matter which ego state she's in, there seems to be a central theme, a common thread to her life."

"Let's talk about the core of human life, the heart of the matter."

Some people seem to express what could be called "personality plus." This is more than just a good personality. It is a vibrancy that is often magnetic. This is because people are more than three P A C circles and the historical people these ego states represent. They are also *themselves*. The "plus" quality is because of the *inner core*. It is a permanent universal reality that underlies the three ego states. When activated, it helps account for some people's boundless energy. From the inner core comes the courage to meet challenges and the motivating force to change.

Watch a television show where people are energized, courageous, and motivated. Use your imagination and guess how this energy (the inner core at work) expresses itself through their:

Parent ego state ______________________________

Adult ego state ______________________________

Child ego state ______________________________

"Every moment seems so full of meaning today."

"My life seems so empty, so lacking in meaning."

"I just can't get going, I feel so listless."

"I feel like I could take the world apart and put it back together in some better way."

"Nothing can stop me now!"

The inner core may be open, so that energy flows easily into each ego state and the meaning of existence is deeply experienced, or it may be blocked, so that energy in one or another ego state is at a low level and life seems to have little meaning.

If you are physically healthy and still find little motivation and energy in your life, your inner core is probably blocked in some way. You are not sufficiently in touch with your body, your mind, and your meanings.

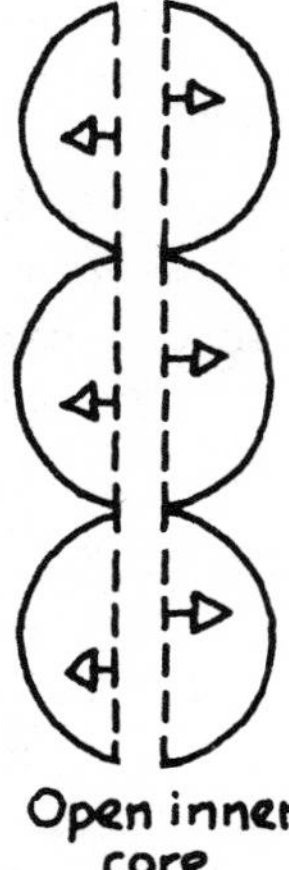

To get in touch with the energy that is blocked or flows freely from your inner core, jot down an important activity in your life — your job, your hobby, your relationships.

____

Record a time when you were full of energy and motivation while engaged in that activity, and another time when you were unenthusiastic and unmotivated about the same thing.

____

Compare your Parent, Adult, and Child responses during those two times.

	Energized and motivated inner core	*Unenergized and unmotivated inner core*
	____________	____________
Parent response	____________	____________
Adult response	____________	____________
Child response	____________	____________

Begin to question yourself about why and how you were energized or not and whether it was related to your courage, your motivation, or your plans. Was it related to the meanings you did or did not find in the activities?

3 All the World's a Stage

The drama script

Even though the human personality may be diagrammed as three ego states with an inner core, people often experience themselves as "wholes" living out, from day to day, a *real life.*

Many films, plays, and television dramas attempt to portray real life. Such shows are often effective because they capture and encapsulate in a short time a story that may have taken months or even years to actually live out.

A good script is the heart of every successful theatrical drama. It brings characters into clear focus, it eliminates any distracting or unnecessary actions, and it identifies the story's theme, or "point," and sticks to it.

A good script allows all the characters to act out their roles completely. Well chosen words and actions heighten the intensity of each character's meaning and purpose. A script may show how characters came to be persecutors, victims, or rescuers. And it tells how the characters turn out in the end, when the final curtain comes down.

Many psychologists — Eric Berne, Fritz Perls, Sidney Jourard, and others — have described people as individuals acting out a script, playing a part on stage, or living out roles. In getting people to think of themselves as actors in a drama on stage, psychologists can help them clarify the roles they play, the themes that commonly run through their daily lives, and the way they use their home and workplace as actors use a stage and setting.

Like actors, many people, knowingly or unknowingly, play roles, wear masks and costumes,and adopt different voices in their lives. They may express themselves simply by "trying to perform adequately," or, as a common expression has it, by "just trying to do my job."

The roles people play can be traced to psychological scripts, which are much like theatrical scripts except that people, unlike actors on a stage, seldom realize they are following a script. They are even less aware of how much their scripts determine their lives — to be constructive, destructive, or going nowhere.

A constructive script signals a basically OK life, full of meaning and purpose, while a destructive script points to a basically not-OK life, where meaning and purpose tend to be lost or distorted. A going-nowhere script is played out by people who live banal existences.

From prologue to final curtain

Scripts people live by, and the stages they select to play them out on, are life plans. Scripts lead to repetitive, compulsive behavior. They often can be recognized when the roles of Victim, Persecutor, and Rescuer are identified.

This chapter helps you get in touch with your script. It shows you how to look at yourself playing the parts your script calls for and how to see life dramas in terms of characters, costumes, settings, plots, actions, and so on, so that you will be effectively equipped to get in touch with your present script and think about a new one.

By doing the exercises in this chapter you will get in touch with elements of the real you and the phony (superficial) you — the you who feels, thinks, and acts from the construc-

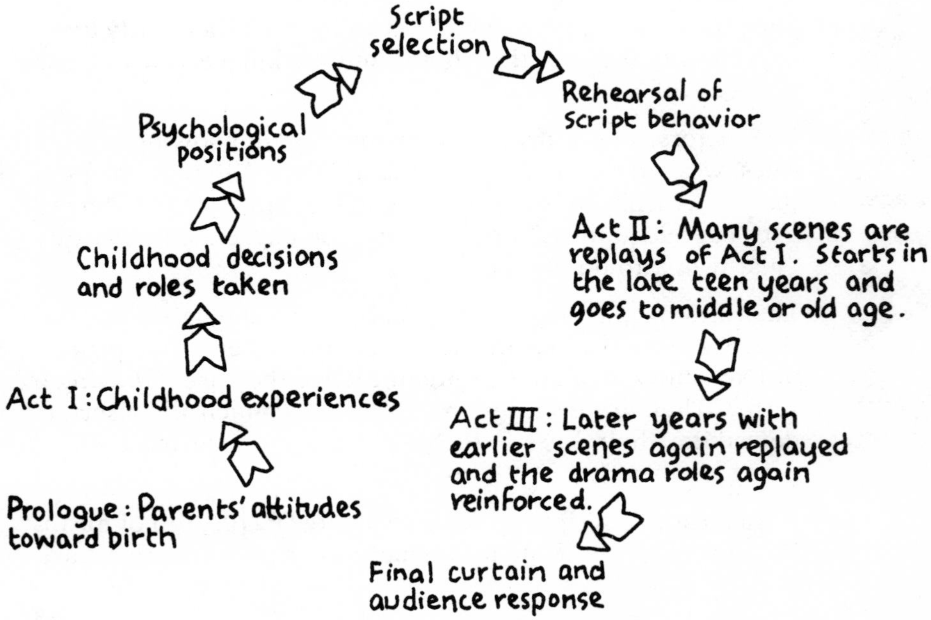

Prologue: Parents' attitudes toward birth

Act I: Childhood experiences

Childhood decisions and roles taken

Psychological positions

Script selection

Rehearsal of script behavior

Act II: Many scenes are replays of Act I. Starts in the late teen years and goes to middle or old age.

Act III: Later years with earlier scenes again replayed and the drama roles again reinforced.

Final curtain and audience response

tive core of the self and the you who feels, thinks, and acts from behind a variety of masks. In a later chapter, you will learn how to rescript yourself and get a new show going more in keeping with your new self. Although details of scenery, dialogue, and characters may change, the drama of your script goes on from birth to death, often with little change.

Who wrote your script?

In script analysis, it is important to remember that each life drama, like every theatrical drama, involves a script, and that *somebody wrote that script.* That "somebody" is you, under the "direction" of your parent figures, who were, of course, influenced by their own background, experience, and parent figures.

If you feel your life is somewhat out of control, or if you don't like where you seem to be going, your life is probably governed by a not-OK script. If you decide to, you can do something constructive about it.

"We need the right scenery to make it work."

"Who will say what to whom?"

"What clothes are needed?"

Shakespeare said all the world is a stage and we are the players on it. Let's imagine that Shakespeare was correct, that people can, indeed, be described as actors in a drama. It is then important for those in charge of the drama to make it a success. And that takes planning. Drama and television producers know how involved and complex putting a play on stage can be.

Imagine you are responsible for producing a successful drama. What would you have to take into account? Make a checklist of at least ten such elements.

________________________ ________________________

________________________ ________________________

________________________ ________________________

________________________ ________________________

________________________ ________________________

Creating a new self is much like producing a new drama. People who want to change themselves can learn a great deal from the drama producer. Now look at the above list and ask yourself if the things on it have anything to do with you and your life. How might you interpret the drama elements in your day-to-day living?

49 *Authenticity and role playing*

"I feel as if I have to put on an act at work."

"She's so phony."

"How can you count on him to be real?"

Play acting is common to everyone. Some people are aware of when and how they do it; others are not. In childhood most children are taught and shown how to act. By the time people are grown up, their actions may reveal personal wholeness and meaning, or they may not. The things people *do* are often related to their vocations or avocations. The *ways* they do them can be authentic or merely role playing.

Think about situations in which you feel as though you have to "put on an act." Putting on an act involves speaking and acting to get other people's attention, approval, or acceptance. Sometimes the "other people" are the internal parents.

Life situations at home or at work where I tend to put on an act	*Life situations where I can be authentic*

"Everyone's always picking on me."

"Let me help you."

"I'll teach you who's boss."

Traditionally, there are three major characters in a drama: (1) the *victim*, who appears to be losing and often wins in the end; (2) the *persecutor*, who is the bad guy and often loses in the end and becomes a victim; and (3) the *rescuer*, who is the good guy yet often is victimized by those who really do not want to be rescued. These possible interactions can be diagrammed as a triangle.[1]

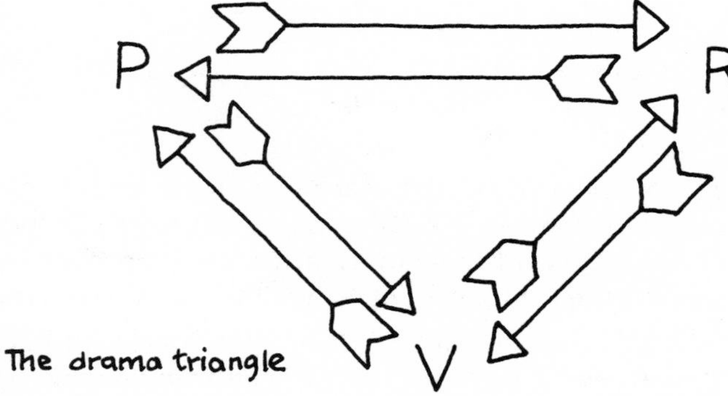

The drama triangle

On life's many stages it is not uncommon for the entire cast of characters to know how to play all the hands in all the games. Each is able to switch and play the three basic roles.[2]

Think of the times when you play each of the three roles: Persecutor, Rescuer, and Victim. List the ways you feel and act that fit the role and keep the drama going.

Roles I act	*Where I play them*	*What I say and do*
________________	________________	________________
________________	________________	________________

"That new hairdo makes you look ten years younger."

"A fashionable suit is the mark of every man in our company."

"I've just got to have a digital wristwatch."

"I couldn't go out of the house without makeup on!"

"She dresses like a gypsy."

In any drama, characters are expected to wear costumes, and sometimes even masks, in order to look the part. Costumes help actors "feel" their roles. The drama may also call for them to use different voices or accents when playing their various parts.

Think of one of the everyday scenes in your life drama. What are some of the costumes and makeup you use when playing your part? Do you use a distinctive voice? Describe how you prepare in the dressing room for your role on stage.

"At home I'm a lover, at work I'm a tyrant."

"I act the same wherever I am."

"My family always lived in big houses."

"The carpet on my office floor makes all the difference."

"If only I had a Cadillac."

Scripts are played out on different stages: at home, at school, at work. Each stage has scenery, props and backdrops, lighting, and sound effects. Each of these elements affects the characters and the audience response.

Think of major areas of your life (home, school, work) as being theatrical. What scenery and props are most valuable to you? What meanings do they hold?

Area of life	*Scenery and props*	*Meaning of the setting*

Suggest some changes in the settings that would let you be more authentic than you now are.

___

___

___

"I keep trying and trying but can't get started."

"If something doesn't work, I stick with it 'til it does."

"Nothing ever seems to turn out right."

"I'll make it. I always do."

All scripts have themes. Procrastinating, succeeding, failing are common script themes. They are usually generated by childhood messages. For example, messages like, "Get all the schooling you can get," or "Money can be used to make money," or "You'll never amount to anything," may determine a script theme for someone.

Think about what happens to you over and over again. That's a script theme. Identify one of your script themes that is "successful," one that is "failing," and one that is "going nowhere" because of procrastinating.

My successful script theme

My failing script theme

My going-nowhere script theme

"I go from one disappointment to another."

"My life is in a tailspin. It's frightening."

"I'm on my way to another new adventure."

"Nothing interesting ever seems to happen here."

"I'm starting another week on the treadmill."

In any drama, the characters have things to say and do. Their actions can be *destructive* of themselves, other people, and relationships; they can be *constructive,* show a vital interest in themselves, other people, and life in general; or they can be *going nowhere,* boring, banal, and repetitive.

In your life drama, what scenes in it are mostly destructive, constructive, or going nowhere? Fill in the blanks with a few concrete examples of your action. At the end of the sentence, put D, C, or G for destructive, constructive, or going nowhere.

When I ______________________________, it is _____.

When I ______________________________, it is _____.

When I ______________________________, it is _____.

When I ______________________________, it is _____.

When I ______________________________, it is _____.

"I wonder who the baby will look like."

"Well, it just *has* to be a boy (girl)."

"I wish we'd never met, then I wouldn't be in this predicament."

In many theatrical dramas, the first act is preceded by a prologue, which serves as a preview or introduction to the play. Notice how on television programs and in theatre dramas, important characters are sometimes mentioned or described before they appear on stage. In life dramas there is always a prologue. This is the first shaping of a life script and takes place even before a child is born. The prologue is the parent's attitudes reflected in their dialogue and action as they anticipate the coming birth of the child.

For your prologue, sit down in a comfortable chair, relax, and imagine what your parents, stepparents, or adopted parents might have done and said in anticipating your birth. Also imagine their response after your birth.

Your parent figures	*Possible feelings about your birth*	*Their possible words about you*	*Their possible feelings and actions toward you after your birth*
________	________	________	________
________	________	________	________
________	________	________	________
________	________	________	________

"When I grow up, I'm going to be a fireman."

"When I grow up, I'll be a nurse."

"I'll get even with him."

In every theatrical drama, the characters are developed in the first act. The theme, or themes, are established through the transactions of the players. The plot begins to unfold according to the script and the roles gradually emerge.

In life scripts, people during early childhood begin to act according to the producer's (the parents') requirements. They learn their "lines," learn how to perform in expected ways, and learn how to play the parts of Rescuer, Persecutor, and Victim.

Fill in the blanks to become aware of your Act I.

I could describe my childhood as ______________________,

______________, ______________, ______________.

Expectations my parents had of me were ______________

____

The theme of my childhood could be summarized in the

words: ______________________________________

My childhood drama parts	*How I played the part*	*With whom*
As Victim	______________	______________
As Rescuer	______________	______________
As Persecutor	______________	______________

"I'm leaving home now and getting my own place."

"Goodbye, Mom and Dad, I'll see you in a year."

"I'm going to get married and start my own life."

In a theatrical drama, the Act I curtain falls when the plot and characters are firmly established. The audience is now interested in what's coming next, if it's good drama. This "what's coming next" is sometimes indicated in the first act — for example, a young person taking piano lessons might look forward to a life involving music.

In a life drama, the curtain on Act I usually falls in late adolescence. By then, the original drama has been tested and rehearsed and assumes a more sophisticated form than in childhood. The lines and roles are familiar to the players.

Consider your teen years, how they were related to your childhood and how the Act I part of your life came to an end. Then fill in the blanks.

The end of my first act came when ______________________.

At that time I was ______________. My predominant feelings

at the time were ______________________________.

As I think about it now I ______________________

____.

At that time, I could see some of "what's coming next" — for

example, ______________________________________.

"If things had been different when I was young, I wouldn't be in this spot now."

"Ever since I was little, I've felt OK."

"Ever since I was a child, I've felt stupid — and often I act that way."

"One day follows another and I get nowhere."

Act II in most people's lives usually starts when they are in their late teens or early twenties, when they start out on their own. The decisions they made in Act I are now revealed in the roles they play and the dramas they act out. One person may choose to be a clown and select a spouse to act as an audience. Another may choose a persecuting role and find other characters to act the part of victim, and so forth. Act II, in many scripts, is a natural development to what happens in the first act.

Get comfortable, close your eyes, and imagine your current life is being shown on a TV screen. Look at yourself in childhood and get in touch with the early decisions you made because of what was going on around you. Then look at yourself as a young adult in the next act of your life. Briefly describe the relationship between your Act I and Act II.

___

___

___

"Just wait and see, I'll lose again. I always do."

"Nobody will ever forget what I've done."

"I want a change of scenery and some new people on my stage."

People who play their roles usually know how they will turn out in the end. They know where they will be each time the curtain falls. Some of you reading this book may be in your teens, thus toward the end of the first act. Many of you are in the middle years of your life, thus in the second act. Some of you are older and in the third act. But all of you can guess how you'll turn out in the end if you keep on going the way you are now. However, at any time in life, if you draw on your urge to live and release the courage from your inner core, you can change your act.

In your mind's eye, see yourself as a character in a play and fill in the following:

What I'll be doing when the curtain on my present act comes

down is: ____

What happens to people like me in my kind of drama is:

____

I could change my story in Act II by doing: ____________

instead of ____________________, which I now do.

"Things are kind of coming to an end for me."

"I'm getting ready to retire now."

"There are a lot of things I wish I had done differently."

"If I had my life to live over again, I'd take some time for me."

For most people, Act III begins roughly between the ages of forty and sixty. It may be because their children have grown up, left home, and established lives of their own. It may be because a spouse or elderly parent has died. Or, it may be because a job has stabilized and there is no challenge in working, or because retirement, with its joys and woes, has arrived.

In Act III of a drama, the action is moving toward resolution. Often the finale can be anticipated, for it seems inevitable in light of the first two acts. It does not need to be that way.

Look at yourself again as though looking at a drama and fill in the following:

For me, Act III is (or will probably be) like ________________

If it is like that, the curtain will come down on a scene of

____

I want Act III to be like ________________________

____

To get what I want, I will need to ________________

____

"I used to think sex was the most important thing for me. I was wrong; it was love, and I let love go."

"Suffering made me see how precious each day is."

"I fought for my kids all the way and I'm glad I did."

"I never earned a million dollars, but I sure had fun."

As people grow older, they often review their lives. Sometimes they are glad for some of the things that happened to them, often they wish things had been different. Looking back on a lifetime, from the perspective of, say, eighty or ninety years of age, they often see more clearly the central meaning and motivating thrust of their lives.

Allow yourself to relax and imagine yourself at a ripe old age, looking back on your life and its meaning. Recall especially: personal achievements and values you worked for; the persons and experiences most meaningful to you; and the suffering you had to endure. Make note of these important events. Note how the central meaning of your life was highlighted by these events and energized by your inner core.

What are some awarenesses you now have of what your new self could be?

Important events	*Meanings the events had or have*	*Inner-core urges involved*
________________	________________	________________
________________	________________	________________
________________	________________	________________
________________	________________	________________

Audience response and critic reviews

"It was well meaning but ineffectual."

"The show was great, I could see it again."

"Ugh. How boring!"

When the final curtain comes down in a theatre, the audience responds — sometimes with enthusiasm, sometimes with disinterest or dissatisfaction. Newspaper and television critics then write reviews, telling what went on and how they evaluate the drama.

In life drama, the audience response and critics' reviews come from friends and foes, family and neighbors. They may indicate it was a good show, well worth watching or being part of, or they may be glad it's over. In any case, the audience response usually reveals whether the drama was phony or authentic.

Imagine you are a theatre critic who writes lengthy, somewhat gossipy, reviews. Write a review of your own drama from this journalist's perspective.

Notes

Process of childhood scripting

Persons who are in the process of creating new selves often are interested in their old selves and "how they got that way." As scripts are part of the old self and have both positive and negative aspects, becoming aware of the how and why such scripts developed often leads to a plan for change.

James and Jongeward, in their book *Born to Win*, outline four steps in creating and maintaining a life script. The steps are:

1. Childhood experiences
2. Days of decision
3. Psychological life positions
4. Script-reinforcing behavior

Childhood experiences, the foundation of everyone's life, shape scripts most significantly. The training, the traumas, the important experiences, the day-by-day routine all contribute to the writing of one's life script. The repeated accusation "you're a sissy" or "you're a coward" may, for example, eventually "script" a person to feel inadequate, or even scared.

The second step, *days of decision* occurring in childhood, also significantly affects a life script. On the basis of traumatic or repeated and reinforced experiences, children often make major decisions at an age when they are far too young to consider things rationally. For example, a child who has the frequent experience of being called "stupid" is likely to decide, "I'm stupid." Often children have little or no control over such influential experiences as the teasing comments of parents, their requests to perform tasks too difficult for their age, the criticisms other siblings use to prove their superiority, and the like. Each such experience may communicate the message, "You're stupid."

Script decisions naturally follow from these consistent or traumatic experiences. Script decisions differ from experiences in that experiences in this context are usually *external*, that is, they arise from sources outside the child and are usually outside the child's control — for example, social situations, public events, unforeseen accidents, the repeated words and actions of parents, teachers, other children, etc. In contrast, *script decisions are always internal and personal.* They are made by the child. They are created from within. Thus, a child reared in relative isolation may decide, "I'm supposed to be a loner," while a child who frequently experiences approval and applause from parents usually decides, "I'm a winner." These decisions mark the second step in shaping a life script.

The *psychological positions* people take toward life are related to their decisions. There are four psychological positions: I'm OK–You're OK; I'm OK–You're not OK; I'm not OK–You're OK; I'm not OK–You're not OK. A child who decides again and again, "I'm stupid," will eventually adopt the *generalized* psychological position, "I'm not OK, other people are OK," and live out that psychological position in an anxious script.

A child who has decided to be a loner usually also decides that other people are not OK. Loners often have fluctuating opinions about their own OKness while living out their lonely script. In contrast, children who receive appropriate approval and encouragement usually hold an I'm OK, You're OK psychological position while living out their loving script.

Script-reinforcing behavior refers to the words and actions that keep a script active. Once a script is selected, people seek to keep their world predictable by reinforcing their script, which means playing the same parts over and over again. The person who decides, "I'm a loner," often chooses a lonely occupation and life style and seeks out other characters who will "keep their distance." Similarly, the person who decides, "I'm stupid, therefore not OK," is likely to reinforce the "stupid" script by *acting* stupid. People will, of course, continue to respond with the "You're stupid" title, and the stupid player will say internally, "I knew it all the time." Thus the drama proceeds predictably scene after scene.

In diagram form, the scripting process of "a clumsy fool" looks like this[1]:

Childhood experiences	Decision	Psychological positions	Script reinforcing behavior
(Being ridiculed for spilling things, falling down, making mistakes)	(I'm clumsy) (My parents will never like me)	(I'm not OK) (They're OK)	(Doing clumsy things and getting ridiculed)

Many people are living out scripts based on decisions they made about their childhood experiences.

Childhood experiences and decisions are also usually intertwined with one's family scripts and the scripts of the larger culture. Members of the Kennedy family, for example, seem to have been scripted for government service, the Curie family for scientific roles, the Martin Luther King family for religious roles.

The following exercises will help you get in touch with the early origins of your script and how this script contributes to the drama you are currently living.

"We from India usually defer to authorities."

"We Japanese have been taught to be polite."

"We in the United States are supposed to make up a melting pot of all peoples, but we don't always melt."

Many cultural traditions are passed on generation after generation from parent to child. These traditions often reflect a racial and ethnic heritage. They include expectations on how people of that culture "should" walk, talk, think, feel, act, succeed, and fail. They are related to jobs, marriage, childrearing practices, and so on. As every person is born into a particular culture, their script usually reflects this heritage.

Select a racial or ethnic group *other than your own.* Describe some of its unique behaviors, as well as meanings these behaviors may have for people in that group. Then, describe your own ethnic/cultural script and its meaning for you.

Other ethnic group

Behavior reflecting a racial or ethnic group	*Meaning it might have for others*
____________________	____________________
____________________	____________________

My ethnic group

Behavior reflecting my cultural scripting	*Meaning it has for me*
____________________	____________________
____________________	____________________

"The kids I go with *all* dress this way."

"Over on our side of town we act differently."

"If I don't join them, they'll beat up on me."

When a culture is large and complex, subcultures exist within it. Subcultures are often defined by geographical location, religious beliefs, age, education, or other common bonds. Each subculture evolves its own dramatic actions. The persons within it may identify themselves by saying "we," and may identify other subcultures by saying "those."

We Southerners	Those Northerners
We under 30	Those over 30
We in this school	Those in that school

Derogatory terms or exaggerations of the speech and mannerisms of others are often used to express subcultural prejudices.[2] Or, prejudice may show in patronizing remarks, such as, "Why, some of my best friends are. . . ."

Human beings are frequently suspicious of differences, and often reflect such mistrust by taking a group position of "We're OK" but — referring to those who are different — "They are not OK." As a result, one group may be pitted against another, each seeing itself as right and the other as wrong. Consequently, antagonism often erupts between subcultural groups.

Consider your national culture and several subcultures you grew up in. Were they compatible or not? ______________

What effects have they had on your life? ______________

____

"Women in our family are always good cooks."

"We've had doctors in our family for three generations."

"I come from a long line of losers."

"Our family genealogy is very interesting."

Cultural and subcultural scripts are often perpetuated through families. Some families, who want to be unique, may fight against these cultural influences; other families may want to be closely identified with their culture and strongly believe that other cultural life styles and values are somehow wrong, even weird.

Like cultural and individual scripts, family scripts may call for action that is constructive, destructive, or banal, thus going nowhere. Some of the most common family scripting messages are related to male and female roles and expectations. Currently many people are evaluating their family scripts and choosing new life styles which, no doubt, will be reevaluated some day by their children and grandchildren.

Think about your family, the way it was when you were growing up, then fill in the lists to see if a script pattern emerges.

Words to describe my family when I was a child	*Expectations for various family members*	*Type of script indicated by pattern*

"You'll always have to take your little sister with you."

"Get your chores done before you play."

"Shut up, or you'll get the back of my hand."

"Don't bother me."

"I'm glad you're you."

The experiences children have with their mothers, fathers, and parenting figures are usually the most influential events in the development of a life script. Sometimes parents, like producers of a theatrical drama, *initiate* some of the positive and negative experiences their children have. Sometimes, like an audience, they *respond,* either positively or negatively, to experiences their children have with others or initiate themselves. Subtle script-reinforcing messages often accompany or underlie their words and actions.

List several people, including your mother, father, foster parents, grandparents, older brothers and sisters, or anyone who had a parenting influence on you when you were young. After each name, write something they said or did that made an impression (for good or ill) on you. Then note what their underlying message was.

Influential people in my childhood	*What they said or did*	*Their underlying message to me*
________________	________________	________________
________________	________________	________________
________________	________________	________________
________________	________________	________________

"You're a Junior and don't forget it."

"I named you after your dear dead brother."

"Your name is unique and sets you apart from the crowd."

"I named you after a popular movie star."

One of the first events that affects a script is the process of being named. The names people have are often related to parental expectations. Names may be clear or ambiguous in regard to gender. They may be common or unusual, easy to pronounce or difficult, popular or odd. In most cases, the names or nicknames that are given to children carry potent messages about the character to be played.

Consider your name, the expectancies it implied, and your feelings and responses.

Name	*Implied message of my name*	*My feelings and responses to my name*
First __________	__________	__________
Middle __________	__________	__________
Last __________	__________	__________
Nickname __________	__________	__________

What I like to be called now: ____________________

This has meaning to me because ____________________

____

____

"When I was six, my father was killed. I miss having a father."

"My mother was an alcoholic. I had to take care of her a lot."

"My uncle used to take me fishing and to ball games."

Childhood experiences are the foundations of a life script. Some events that affect people include: death or illness in the family, moving to a new place, being in an accident, living in an isolated situation, living in a crowded situation, extreme poverty, being an only child, being one of many children, unusual vacations, special gifts, divorced parents, loud arguments, joyous parties, etc.

List significant events in your life, especially those that happened in childhood. Note your approximate age when the event happened. Whenever possible, connect the event in some way to what keeps happening to you over and over, or to what you work hard to avoid repeating. For example, if you had an alcoholic parent you might have chosen an alcoholic spouse, and the same scenes may reoccur in your current life. Or you may shun people who drink as though they had the plague.

My age then	*The significant event*	*Connection with my script*
______	____________________	____________________
______	____________________	____________________
______	____________________	____________________

"Stand up for your rights."

"Don't let anyone tell you they're better than you are."

"Keep your body clean."

"We don't talk about sex in this house."

"Keep a little fun in your life."

Children are constantly hearing directions from others about how they *should* live their lives. These messages often have a lasting impact on a child's life script.

Make note of some message you remember receiving during childhood concerning the following topics. What was your reaction?

	Message received during childhood	*Its effect on me*
Being a man	______________	______________
Being a woman	______________	______________
Taking care of my body	______________	______________
Sex and sexuality	______________	______________
Relaxation, enjoyment, fun	______________	______________

"I'll never trust anyone again."

"I'll never make it, no matter what."

"People like me."

"I can always get a man by being sexy."

"I'll get by with a little bit of luck."

Childhood decisions are usually responses to childhood experiences. While experiences are usually due to external events, decisions are always internal and personal. For example, if mother or father dies when a child is young, and if the child does not have a loving substitute, that child feels abandoned and usually decides not to get close to or trust people of the same sex as the parent who died. The child assumes, "If I love people they will go away." Choosing a life script is a childhood decision that often represents a turning point in a person's life.

Note some decisions you made, especially when you were young, that helped point you in the direction of your life script. Note your approximate age at the time of the decision and how the decision may have influenced your life script.

Age	*Decisions I made about myself*	*How it influenced my life script later*
______	____________________	____________________
______	____________________	____________________
______	____________________	____________________

"My parents always said I'd be a dancer."

"My folks pressured me to go to college, but I refused to go."

"I won't be a lawyer like my father."

"Like mom says, a woman's place is in the home."

"I'm expected to carry on the family business. What else can I do?"

Perhaps the most important decision a child makes in the face of parental suggestions about a life script is to comply or to rebel. Some people compliantly act out the scripts selected for them; others fight this parental typecasting. Many people who would like to rebel choose to *procrastinate*. This is a partial compliance maneuver that communicates the message, "I'll probably do it your way, but not exactly as you want it and not for a while."

List some script messages your mother, father, or other parent figures gave you and indicate how you responded to their expectancies.

Scripting messages	*Person who was the source of scripting*	*How I complied, rebelled, or procrastinated*

"I find people interesting and fun."

"I'm the boss in this house."

"I never do anything quite right."

"I'm always getting criticized."

"I can't trust anyone in this place."

Early in life, people usually assume one of four general positions toward life as a whole:

- *Confident (I'm OK — You're OK)* people tend to accept themselves and others as responsible, interesting, and fun
- *Superior (I'm OK — You're not OK)* people tend to put themselves on top and to put others down
- *Anxious (I'm not OK — You're OK)* people feel inadequate and compare themselves negatively with others
- *Hopeless (I'm not OK — You're not OK)* people tend to lose faith in others and have no hopes or expectations.

Which of the four general life-as-a-whole positions were you cast in as a child? Check one.

( ) Confident ( ) Superior ( ) Anxious ( ) Hopeless

How would this life position reinforce your present role?

"I'm just an ugly duckling."

"I've always dreamed of being superman."

"I'm waiting for my prince to come."

"Eleanor Roosevelt always inspired me."

"Do you know the story of the famous spy?"

Children usually have favorite fairy tales or stories that they want to hear over and over again. Frequently, such stories are related to a child's life script and present a summary of the drama the child may desire to live out in the years ahead.

Recall your favorite childhood story or fairytale.

Which characters in it do you strongly respond to — either positively or negatively?

How are these characters like you, or unlike you, in the way they live?

The play goes on

"You be the mommy and I'll be the daddy."

"She'll grow up to be a doctor."

"I'm going to be the teacher. You sit down and do what I say."

"Isn't his mind amazing; he'll make a fine scientist."

Some people are surprised to find out how young they were when they began following their script. Scripting for a vocation often occurs because grownups talk *about* children in their presence. Grownups also instruct children *directly* about their vocations and the parts they think each child should play.

You might like to discover how long you've been playing the part you now play in the selection of your vocation. Close your eyes and imagine that the drama of your early life is being projected on a movie screen in front of you. See and hear once more the significant people in your life talking *to* you or *about* you and your life script. Now list about four or five statements that you can recall, and your reactions to them.

What people said to me or about me	*How I felt about what they said*	*What I did about what they said*
________________	________________	________________
________________	________________	________________
________________	________________	________________
________________	________________	________________

"I read in the newspaper that everyone has criminal tendencies."

"My teacher told me that I was very logical."

"I met an old friend today and she liked the way I looked."

"I've learned a lot from watching television."

"People expect me to be dressed nicely."

In a dramatic production, certain members of the crew never come on stage — for example, the prompter, the cue-giver, or the stage manager — but these individuals do give directions to people on stage. In real life, off-stage directors may include friends, siblings, teachers, neighbors, the books and magazines we read, the television programs we watch, and so on.

List "off-stage" messages you received as a child. Put an L or D after each to indicate whether you liked or disliked the message.

Off-stage childhood directions	*From whom*	*Liked or disliked*
________	________	____
________	________	____
________	________	____
________	________	____
________	________	____
________	________	____

The reinforced script

"Why does this always happen to me?"

"Every time I get involved with a man, I wind up feeling hurt."

"This job is no different from the others — I can't seem to get promoted."

"Not this same old act again!"

Scripts are chosen in childhood. They are based on early experiences and decisions and are reflected in psychological positions. Later in life, the script is acted out, over and over again. The actors interact in expected ways, saying the same words, playing the same parts they learned when they were young. Scripts are reinforced by repetitive behavior, brief vignettes that are, in fact, replays of earlier scenes.

Describe an important childhood event: ____________________

____

Describe similar experiences in your life that appear to be a replay of the childhood event: ____________________

____

If you don't like the "replays" of earlier acts, what would you need to do to avoid them? ____________________

____

5 Contracting for a New Self

People aware of their need for self-change may say, "The way I used to act and feel just doesn't make sense anymore. I'm changing and I want to do it consciously. I really want to learn how to be healthier — physically as well as emotionally. I want a new self, and I want to be aware of what's happening to me as I change."

People who think like this are embarking on an exciting internal adventure, and yet the road to self-discovery is not an easy one. It requires courage, motivation, and a plan.

Many people seem to have most of the required ingredients for a successful self-change. They have goals, they are willing to change things in themselves, and they are courageous and motivated. Yet, when they get to the step-by-step planning stage, they get stuck. Their plans may prove too vague and unrealistic, or too demanding and unreasonable, or too complicated and involved. For such people, self-contracts are helpful. Even people who do not feel stuck often can use contracts to further develop a new self.

A new kind of plan

A self-contract is a new kind of plan, one of the simplest, most effective, and versatile TA tools for self-change. Learning how to use the self-contract format and draw up contracts is the goal of this chapter.

A self-contract may be a new idea to some people since the word "contract" usually connotes an agreement between two or more people. Contracts between people are, of course, the most common contract form. People sign work contracts with employers to change their salaries; they enter marriage contracts with spouses to exchange certain rights and privileges; they sign mortgage contracts with banks to change the house they live in. People make contracts-of-purchase with department stores, contracts-of-credit with credit-card companies, contracts-of-savings with banks, and so on.

In a similar way, when people want to make a personal change in themselves, it is helpful for them to enter into a self-contract.

Self-contracts and contracts are both, in one way or another, *agreements to change (or exchange) something.* A self-contract is an agreement you make with yourself to change something about yourself. It may be entered into by such expressions as, "I promise myself to . . . ," or "I choose to . . . ," or "I contract with myself to. . . ."

In self-therapy, a person exchanges his or her present self for a new self. A shy person, for example, can make a self-contract to develop a more forward and assertive self; a chronic complainer can contract to exchange a critical self for a complimenting self; or someone who presently feels guilty when saying "no" can contract to exchange for a new self who can say "no" and feel OK about it.

Self-contracts were designed for people who believe that they can change their appearance, their behavior, their feelings, and their attitudes, and that these changes can enhance their lives.

Self-contracts first focus on the general areas where change is desired (improving appearance, gaining competence, lowering blood pressure, etc.). Next, specific goals (gaining or losing weight, getting a degree in school, learning how to do something new, etc.) are established. Faced with various avenues for achieving their goals, self-contract makers then learn how to select those options that are reasonable, practical, and measurable, and they enter into a self-contract.

Be your own lawyer

Self-contracts also need to include protective elements, such as time limits, sanctions, opportunities for revision, and the privilege of breaking the contract. Such terms are included in every well-designed contract.

Lawyers design contracts in the best interests of their clients, carefully analyzing each term of a contract, watching for loopholes, and in general protecting their client's interests. In self-therapy, you will be your own lawyer, since you will be asked to draw up your own contracts. This chapter is designed to show you how to become an expert at constructing effective self-contracts for self-therapy.

If, for one reason or another, your contract fails to work, you can learn to revise it, rewrite it, or creatively design a new contract — one that is realistic, has the possibility of being achieved, contributes to your desired new self, and adds meaning to your life.

The self-contract–making process is summarized at the end of the chapter in a comprehensive, easy-to-use self-contract formula. When followed, this formula offers better chances than ever for successfully implementing your plan for self-change. You can use the formula again and again in different ways and at different times. In fact, the entire process of unfolding a new self may be described as fulfilling a series of self-contracts that will enhance and enrich your life.

"I wish I could relate better to my children."

"I wish I were more patient with myself."

"I wish I could afford to send the kids to college."

"I've always wanted to find the real purpose to my life."

Just about everybody would like to be a little bit better or to experience life more fully. Almost everyone can list things they feel would improve or enhance life. Some desire *material* improvements, such as a new car, more money, a decent place to live, and the like. Others look for more *personal* ways to improve. They seek to develop their minds and personalities, to improve their health, and to release energies hidden in their inner core. Still others look for a *philosophy* to live by or a new purpose in their lives. These desires and wishes may be generalized or specific. When they become specific and plans are made to achieve them, energy, excitement, and enthusiasm are released.

List some of the desires and wishes you have at this time, especially those that would enhance your life.

"My problem is my relationship with my mother."

"Something's gotta be done about my high blood pressure."

"I need a new interest now that I've retired."

"Home life is just food and TV for me."

Successful self-contracts, like good business contracts, start by focusing on one general area of personal concern. Contracts that are too broad in scope are likely to fail because they are too complicated, or too vague, or can't be revised with ease. Better to make a number of small contracts than one of cosmic proportions.

Areas of personal concern commonly include physical appearance, personal habits, interpersonal situations that generate pain and hurt, job satisfaction, family life, education, health, use of leisure time, becoming more competent, having more fun, discovering more meaning.

At this time, what are some *general* areas about which you might wish to make self-contracts?

____

____

____

____

____

____

____

A particular goal

"I want more fun in my life."

"I want to get in touch with my feelings."

"I want to stop being afraid of people."

"I want to learn to play tennis."

Once the general area of concern for change has been defined, it helps to become more specific and say, for example, "What I want to accomplish is. . . ." Such formulations help focus inner-core energies. People concerned about their physical appearance might describe their *specific* goal in terms of *wanting to lose ten pounds.* Those interested in their interpersonal relations might describe their goal in terms of *wanting to have three new friends.*

Effective people have goals in mind before they enter into contracts. They know ahead of time *specifically* what they want.

Look back at what you wrote for the last exercise, select one area of concern, and evaluate its importance to you.

One of the things I really want is ______________________

What I might gain from it is ______________________

What I might lose if I get it is ______________________

Consequently I ______________ (do or do not) want it ______________ (more or less)

than I originally believed.

If you conclude you don't really want this goal, go through this exercise again, beginning with one of your other desires.

"To rest my feet I could stand on my head."

"To get more money I could become a counterfeiter."

"To be a better friend I could talk less (or more)."

Frequently, people are fully aware of their areas of concern and can also formulate their personal goals and objectives in each area. But they seem to reach an impasse when it comes to spelling out concrete and specific ways to face their challenges or problems. Sometimes, imagination and creativity are called for.

Brainstorming, a simple technique designed to release people's creativity, is commonly used by corporation "think tanks," where the goal is often to find a new solution for an old problem. While brainstorming, people avoid value judgments and evaluations. They list all ideas, regardless of how irrational or impractical the ideas may seem. This stimulates further creativity and more ideas. Brainstorming is fun, it's fast, and it often provides new and surprising solutions.

Fill in the following blanks quickly, giving free rein to your creativity and *not* stopping to evaluate what you write.

A personal goal I have or problem I want to solve is ______

____.

Possible solutions are ______________________,

and ______________________, and ______________________,

and ______________________, and ______________________,

and ______________________, and ______________________.

Reasonable, practical, measurable

"I agree to lose ten pounds a week." (unreasonable)

"I agree to lose one pound per week." (reasonable)

"I agree to work toward a better world." (impractical)

"I agree to volunteer my services at the Red Cross for six months." (practical)

"I agree to cut down on my smoking in the future." (nonmeasurable)

"I agree to smoke only twelve cigarettes per day this week." (measurable)

Many people formulate desired changes in ways that are unreasonable, impractical, and nonmeasurable. Such self-contracts are doomed to fail simply because they cannot be carried out, or because the do-er has no means of measuring success.

Before business negotiators are satisfied with the wording of a contract, they may rewrite it a dozen times, always looking for the precise words to make the contract say exactly what they want it to say. Even expert lawyers often spend long hours trying to find the "right words." (So do authors like ourselves!) People who write self-contracts will discover that it takes time to formulate a success-oriented contract.

Take your specific objective and translate it into an agreement with yourself that is reasonable, practical, and measurable. Rewrite it several times if necessary.

"I agree to lose one pound every week, even if it makes me miserable."

"I'm going to quit smoking — cold turkey — I'm not going to like it."

"It delights me to think about this change."

"I feel a little uneasy about this contract."

Uncooperative emotions can block a contract's success, so people need to ask themselves questions like: Does this contract seem excessively harsh or threatening? Would my emotions help me stick to the self-contract I've made?

State some emotions or feelings that you experience when you present your self-contract to yourself.

If you find little or no strong emotional support for your self-contract, consider revising it until the statement "feels good inside" when you say it.

"I've got a lot of willpower."

"That new dress will motivate me to diet."

"People tell me I'm basically kind and loving."

Many self-contracts fail because helpful personal resources are not recognized or used. Business people call upon their personal and corporate resources to carry out a contract effectively. In fact, contract deadlines and stipulations usually demand the full and efficient use of resources. Similarly, in self-contracting, the more skills, talents, abilities, and native gifts people can call upon, the better.

List the personal resources that you feel would or could help bring about a successful completion of your self-contract.

My resources	*How I might use them to help*
____________________	____________________
____________________	____________________
____________________	____________________

Now use the power of your imagination and brainstorm resources you might have but not use, and that you could develop.

My potential resources	*How I might develop them*
____________________	____________________
____________________	____________________
____________________	____________________

"I put a quarter in this jar every time I resist criticizing the children."

"I keep a graph to note my improvement in swimming."

"I mark an X on my calendar whenever I'm first to smile or say 'hello'."

"I give myself a special treat whenever I get an A or B on math tests."

The saying, "Nothing succeeds like success," is also true in self-contracting. Periodically, business people call for a progress report to see if the step-by-step elements of the contract are being adhered to. They want to know if the contract is proceeding "on schedule." In self-contracting, a calendar may be used to keep a daily self-contract progress report, or you may offer yourself a reward for each successful step along the way.

Note some ways you could measure the success of your contract. A *measurable* self-contract will usually offer visible ways to measure progress.

Ways I could measure my progress

________________________ ________________________

________________________ ________________________

"I'll know I've made it when I step on the scale and it reads 112 pounds."

"By next Friday, my checklist will prove that I did everything I promised to."

"I'll know I've fulfilled my contract when I have 30 quarters in the jar."

"My graph will tell me whether or not I've succeeded."

Self-contracts, like business contracts, usually state clearly the goal of the contract and the time limits on the agreement. Business people who write contracts without clear goals, or without schedules and deadlines, soon find themselves without a business. Without a schedule and a clear goal, a self-contract is also likely to end up alongside last year's unfulfilled New Year's resolutions.

State how you will know when your self-contract is fulfilled. Include the time limits.

____

____

If you cannot, perhaps you'll need to revise the way you've stated your self-contract to make it more measurable. Rewrite it here.

____

____

____

"The times I really have to watch my weight is when I'm home alone with nothing to do and I nibble."

"I tend to be naggy at nights. It's my worst time."

"It's after a hard day that I usually give up being kind and I simply get angry at her."

"Years of bad habits will probably come back to plague me."

One of the best defenses a military general has against defeat is to know the enemy and his tactics. In self-contracting, people can be their own worst enemies. A self-contract can be sabotaged from within.

What are the times, places, and situations when you are most likely to weaken in observing your self-contract?

1. ____________________ 3. ____________________

2. ____________________ 4. ____________________

Can you think of ways to deal with these special situations when they arise?

1. ____________________ 3. ____________________

2. ____________________ 4. ____________________

"A penny saved is a penny earned."

"If at first you don't succeed, try, try again."

"Don't rock the boat."

"Don't cry over spilt milk."

Parent messages received in childhood and incorporated into the Parent ego state may help a self-contract succeed, especially if parental values, traditions, life styles, etc. tend to support the chosen self-contract. Parental training may also undermine a self-contract in subtle ways, so it is helpful to be in touch with your inner Parent to see if its support can be elicited or not. Without inner Parent support, people need more courage and higher motivation to succeed in fulfilling their self-contracts.

List what you imagine your parents would say about the changes you now want to make. Recall some of their mottos, or favorite sayings, or how their actions reflected their basic attitudes about change. List those that might give inner support to your contract, as well as those that might undermine it.

My parental opinions on the kind of change I want to make	*Supportive or non-supportive of my change*
____________________	____________________
____________________	____________________
____________________	____________________
____________________	____________________

"If I try, it won't be good enough."

"Why should I work so hard, no one else does."

"I'll do it later."

Fear of not succeeding, anger at what seems unfair, and procrastination because of a lack of interest are only three of the many ways the Child ego state can contaminate the Adult and sabotage the desired goal of a self-contract.

Procrastination isn't always sabotage. People who procrastinate in making decisions or taking action sometimes do so in order to collect necessary information to make a rational decision. More often, though, procrastination simply masks the inner Child's fear, anger, rebellion, or hostility.

List experiences, training, habit patterns, or feelings that you learned as a child. Focus on those that relate to your self-contract. Then, consider how each item might influence your desired change.

Childhood experiences	*Would help or hinder*	*In what ways*
______________	______________	______________

Childhood training	*Would help or hinder*	*In what ways*
______________	______________	______________

Childhood feeling	*Would help or hinder*	*In what ways*
______________	______________	______________

Should I tell?

"If I tell her about my diet, she'll make me stick to it."

"I'm going to ask the people at the office to remind me when I curse or swear."

"My self-contract must be hidden from everyone."

"If I told him, he'd ruin the whole project."

Sometimes it's helpful for others to know about a self-contract, sometimes it isn't. Telling or not telling others may be a subtle form of sabotage.

Even in business, some contracts need to be kept secret, for their success depends on an element of "surprise." On the other hand, the success of some contracts may be enhanced when they are made public.

In self-contracting, the person making the contract needs to consider whom to tell and when it would be helpful to tell.

Who, knowing my self-contract, might help me fulfill it?	*Who, knowing my self-contract, might hinder its fulfillment?*
________________	________________
________________	________________
________________	________________

What I could do with those people who might hinder my self-contract is ______________________________.

Therefore I will ____________________ to avoid sabotage.

"You look fantastic. You've lost at least a dozen pounds."

"I'll simply tell my husband that I'm going to compliment the children every day."

"My boss will be the first to notice the change, and she'll be delighted."

"He would never notice a thing like this, unless it appeared in the newspaper headlines."

In time, people will begin to recognize that you have changed. That's inevitable.

When other people begin to notice a change, they might respond to you in new ways. They may even comment about the changes they observe.

Business people, usually happy to let others know of their successes, utilize advertising, promotion, and public relations as ways of announcing their organization's progress. Success brings new customers, new contracts, and bigger profits. Similarly, successful self-contracting encourages further progress in shaping a new self.

How will other important people in your life come to know about the change you're making? Will they discover it for themselves? How? Will you have to tell them? What might their reactions be when they find out?

Person involved	*How they'll come to know*	*Their possible reactions to my change*
______________	______________	______________
______________	______________	______________
______________	______________	______________

"My self-contract to get a raise here is impossible — our company's going bankrupt."

"It's a bit ambiguous, but I think it will clear up in a month."

"I can change my contract a dozen different ways."

"My plan is as simple as counting from one to ten."

When self-contracts are not initially well formulated, or become impossible to fulfill, or lose their original meanings, a revision is necessary. Some people try doggedly to live up to a self-contract when it really is beyond their powers to accomplish.

Good business people are aware of their limits. They know that a contract too big for them may do more harm than good to their company. They also wisely design contracts that are not too rigid, that allow room for bargaining and revision. They know that situations change and such factors often necessitate changing contracts.

Consider some of the "New Year Resolutions" you have made in the past. Did you keep them, keep trying, or give them up?

New Year Resolutions	*What I did about them*
______________________	______________________
______________________	______________________
______________________	______________________

Now think about your contract or contracts.

Contracts I have	*What I might do*	*Possible revisions*
______________	______________	______________
______________	______________	______________

The long form of the self-contract asks you all the important questions that need to be answered before making an effective self-contract. Hopefully, it covers most of the usual loopholes. If you get stuck at a particular step, go back and reread the exercise related to that step. The page number of the corresponding exercise follows each statement.

1. What I want that would enhance my life is ____________

   ____ (86)

2. The general area or areas of my life that this desire

   reflects is ______________________________________ (87)

3. The way I could describe my desired goal more precisely

   is ____ (88)

4. Ways I could work on this are ____________________

   ____ (89)

5. What *I* would need to *change,* stated practically, reasonably, and measurably is ______________________

   ____ (90)

6. What I am *willing* to do to effect the change is ______

   ____ (90)

7. How I'd need to restructure my time and priorities is

   ____ (90)

8. Personal skills, talents, abilities, and native gifts I have that would help me keep this contract and effect this

   change are _______________________________________

   ____ (92)

9. My Parent values, traditions, prejudices, or life styles

   might support or sabotage my contract by ____________

   ____ (96)

10. The ways this contract appeals to my Child or seems too hard or threatening to my Child feelings are ____________ ______________________________ (97)

11. I can evaluate my *progress* in achieving my contract by ______________________________ ______________________________ (93)

12. I'll know my self-contract is *fulfilled* when ____________ ______________________________ (94)

13. I might sabotage my self-contract by ____________ ______________________________ (95)

14. *Others* will come to know about the change I'm making if I ______________________________ (99)

15. Some others, knowing about my contract might help or hinder its fulfillment or effectiveness. (98)

Who might help	*Who might hinder*
____________	____________
____________	____________
____________	____________

16. What I could do about people who might *hinder* me is ______________________________ ______________________________ (98)

17. The ways I could get people to *help* me are ____________ ______________________________ ______________________________ (98)

18. If my self-contract needed revision, I could revise it by

____ (100)

19. What I can learn if my contract doesn't work, regardless of how courageous and motivated I am, regardless of how carefully I've planned, is _______________

____

20. When I look back at what I wrote to the first question I think the meaning it reflects in my life is related to ____

____
(personal achievements, positive experiences, or unavoidable suffering)

21. As I think this over I feel _______________ and I conclude _______________________________________

22. Now, having explored various facets related to my goal, my agreement to change (my self-contract), stated reasonably, practically, and measurably is _____________

____

____

____

____

Self-contract: short form

People can follow the long form of the self-contract in any area of their lives that they wish to change. In time, and with practice, a shorter form may be used just as effectively.

Only five questions are used in the short form. If you happen to get stuck at one of the questions or feel confused in the process, then review the longer self-contract form related to your trouble spot.

1. What I want that would enhance my life is ____________

   ____.

2. What I would need to change to get it is ____________

   ____.

3. What I'm *willing* to do to make it happen is ____________

   ____.

4. Others would know about the change I'm making when or

   if I ____.

5. I might sabotage myself by ____________________________

   ____.

6. Therefore, my agreement to change (my self-contract), stat-

   ed reasonably, practically, and measurably is ____________

   ____.

7. When I achieve my contract, the meaning it will give my

   life is ____.

Notes

6 Self Re-Adulting

Requirements for re-Adulting

Your Adult, motivated by the power within you — the urge to live a life full of meaning — is potentially your strongest ally. If it is uncontaminated, flexible, and updated with current information, your Adult is like a strong referee in a boxing match. It will separate the negative aspects of your Parent and Child and insist on fair play. It will use the positive aspects of your Parent and Child to enhance your life and the lives of others.

The Adult ego state is *somewhat* like a muscle. It increases in strength with exercise. The Adult ego state is also *somewhat* like a computer. Like a computer, it can be fed misinformation and thus make erroneous decisions.

People who are constantly Adult have overly strong ego-state boundaries around their Adult. Consequently, their energy does not flow easily throughout their personalities. They are objective and impersonal, much like a machine.

In contrast, people with weak Adult ego state boundaries have contaminated opinions and feelings — they are overdominated by their Child and Parent ego states. Such people may often be tired, physically and emotionally, because their Adult, like a weak muscle or like an inadequate referee, does not control the continuous Parent-Child inner dialogue.

Both those with rigid boundaries around their Adult and those with weak ones need self re-Adulting. The goal of re-Adulting is to integrate the personality so that the Adult is not functioning merely like a mechanistic computer or like an

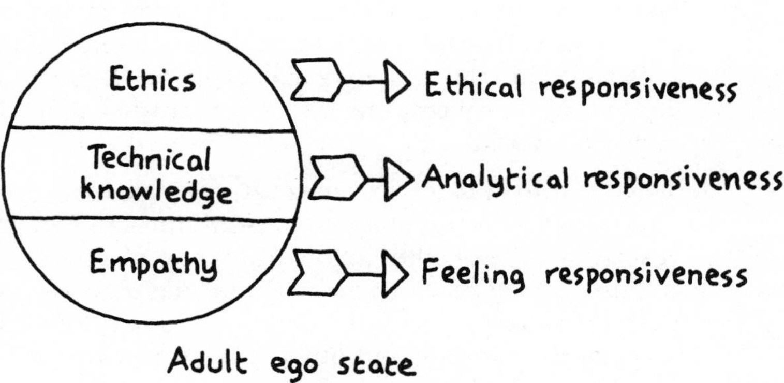

under- or overdeveloped muscle. Rather, the goal is to release the Adult's capacity for directing the entire personality in such a way that it can call on the emotionally healthy Child and the emotionally healthy Parent ego states.

The three parts of the integrated Adult ego state are illustrated in the accompanying diagram.

A lifelong process of growth

Naturally, the self re-Adulting process takes courage, motivation, and planning. As a result, it usually expands into an exciting lifelong process of growth.

The two most common hindrances in this growth process are contamination or rigidity. Many people need to *decontaminate* the Adult by learning how to collect accurate information and keeping it updated. Others need to *relax* their ego state boundaries so that the boundaries are permeable and, as persons, they become more flexible and less addicted to a particular ego state.

When these problems are solved, the Adult can become integrated. The ethical Parent responses and the empathetic Child responses can flow into the Adult and be directed outward to enhance the quality of life.

Re-Adulting calls for (1) realignment of ego state boundaries in contaminated areas, or relaxation of ego state boundaries if the Adult is too "thick skinned"; (2) updating information and skills through a continuous education program, including the use of current facts in the here and now; and (3) integration within the total personality of the OK parts of the Parent and Child by creating permeable, rather than rigid, ego state boundaries.

Thus, to fully integrate your Adult, you, like most people, may also need to do some healthy re-Childing, re-Parenting, and rescripting (see the following three chapters). For this reason, the self re-Adulting process is necessarily first. As you develop a stronger ethical, empathetic, and informed Adult to serve as ally, friend, and inner therapist, you will be able to do the self re-Parenting, re-Childing, and rescripting that follows.

Broader horizons

As the personality becomes more healthily integrated, it becomes less focused on itself and more open to social values and other broader horizons.[1] People who have integrated Adult ego states experience meaning in all spheres of existence. They feel within themselves a strong urge to live, to be free, to relate in meaningful ways to others and to their natural environment. They want to experience and analyze situations, and make and carry out their decisions. This is the energy from the inner core — the universal self — unifying them to become fully human.

"When not at work, I read technical journals."

"Watching TV newscasts keeps me informed."

"In many situations I feel awkward, as though I lack ordinary social skills."

"I treat my employees differently, as each is a unique person."

The Adult acts as the information center of the self, collecting, evaluating, and processing data from the inner and outer worlds. This exercise tests to see if an Adult ego state needs exercise in information gathering from the *outer* world. Collecting accurate information facilitates decontamination.

Check those that apply to you.

( ) I find that I frequently confuse information that I read or hear from others.

( ) I find that I often give a distorted picture of information when I tell it to someone.

( ) I often can't find a reasonable answer or a helpful suggestion to give to others when one is called for.

( ) At times I can't tell whether my language and behavior are appropriate in a certain situation.

( ) I sometimes make decisions when the facts aren't really complete and clear — and they could be.

If you checked any of the above boxes, you may want to develop a self-contract to do something about your Adult's ability to collect data from the outer world.

In touch with the outer world

"I spend hours trying to figure myself out."

"I like being alone with myself."

"I'm always panicky and scared."

"I don't understand why I do what I do."

"I wonder how to feel more competent."

Within the self, the Adult differentiates Parent, Adult, and Child responses. It evaluates these responses as reliable and appropriate here and now. It also notices ego-state patterns and habits.

Check those that apply to you.

( ) I experience inner dialogue conflicts frequently and I have no idea what to do about them.

( ) In some situations my responses are usually unpredictable.

( ) I find it almost impossible to distinguish Parent or Child responses, in either others or myself.

( ) I find it difficult to formulate practical and measurable self-contracts.

( ) I find it difficult to design ways of behaving that allow the Child to have its way and the Parent to feel respected.

( ) I seldom make plans before I begin a project. I prefer simply to plunge right in.

If you checked any of the above, you may want to develop a self-contract to do something about your Adult's ability to collect data from the inner world.

"Some people laugh much louder than others."

"My boss's writing is sometimes hard to read."

"He often says, 'Make it brief,' and that's not easy."

"I keep working on things until they're right."

"She waves her hands so much when she talks that I stand back."

As a data collector, the Adult gathers information about kinds of behavior that offer new ways of thinking about people, feelings, and events. The Adult gathers data by observing others, by reading, by going to school, etc.

Recall the way you do the activities listed below. Observe how others do the same activity. Look for differences.

Activity	*What I do*	*What others do*
Getting a new job	________________	________________
Reacting to strangers	________________	________________
Laughing	________________	________________
Explaining a new idea	________________	________________
Gesturing with hands	________________	________________
Learning something new	________________	________________

"It doesn't have to always be my way."

"I'm willing to admit I'm sometimes wrong."

"I could learn how to hook rugs."

"It's interesting to experiment with styles of writing."

"I'd like to try a new restaurant."

"Let's see how I look with a new hair style."

When tempted to be overly rational, the Adult, as governor of the personality, may hesitate to allow Parent and Child enough freedom to express themselves. To develop flexibility in the use of all three ego states, the Adult may explore situations where Parent and Child responses may be encouraged.

Think over your behavior during the past 24 hours. Do you feel that the interplay of your three ego states was pretty well balanced, that is, was each ego state getting plenty of opportunity to express itself?

Think of new (or presently unused) ways in which your Child could become more fully involved in your life. Do the same for your Parent and your Adult.

New Child responses	*New Parent responses*	*New Adult responses*
________________	________________	________________
________________	________________	________________
________________	________________	________________
________________	________________	________________

"I'll get it if I keep working on it."

"Sometimes I fail the first time and succeed later."

"It's like learning to walk — it takes practice."

"Focusing on the problem may lead to some answers."

Frequently the Adult needs practice in gathering accurate information. A weak Adult may need to learn how to concentrate better, even when the concentration seems like a chore.

If your Adult is particularly weak in gathering information from the outer world, experiment with the following.

- Watch some person for about an hour (someone on a television show, for example) and list their P, A, C expressions. Try to collect at least ten expressions from each ego state.

If you need to practice self-observation, try the following.

- Monitor your own conversation for about an hour (record yourself on a tape cassette, if you have one, and listen to the playback). Collect at least ten expressions from each ego state. If your attention wanders, remind yourself of your need to learn how to concentrate.

"I balanced the check book the first time around."

"I like the way I solved that problem."

"Actually, I'm an excellent teacher."

"As a person, I'm fun, trustworthy, and I have a sharp mind."

One of the ways your Adult has of evoking full cooperation among ego states is by giving positive recognition to yourself whenever you utilize their capacities. Positive self-reinforcement is especially valuable in the face of emotional despair, physical pain, or low motivational energy.

List the positive statements you can honestly make about your Child and your Parent.

Affirming my Child	*Affirming my Parent*
________________	________________
________________	________________
________________	________________

Also make a list of your self-therapy "wins," no matter how small. These are affirmations for your Adult.

________________ ________________

________________ ________________

Positive recognition helps reenergize the personality and encourages perseverance in self-therapy when the going gets rough.

"Maybe I need to try a different approach."

"What are some other possibilities?"

"Every day doesn't have to be the same."

"What might other people suggest?"

One of the benefits of data gathering is discovering new response options, alternative ways of behaving, and ideas you've never tried before. In designing self-contracts, the Adult often needs to create options and alternatives until one is found that both pleases the Child and is approved by the Parent.

Think of some situation, activity, or relationship in your life that is "in a rut." Suggest two or three alternative approaches that would please the Child and meet with Parent approval.

How am I in a rut? ____________________

Alternative approaches to please my Child ____________________

____

____

Alternative approaches my Parent would approve of ____________________

____

____

____

"I can't please anyone or do anything right."

"Failure is my middle name."

"There I go again, as usual."

"Why ever work if I don't have to?"

"I'll wait a while, then I'll get even."

The Adult recognizes inappropriate responses in the Child and the need for re-Childing. In self re-Childing, the Adult locates the problem's source and suggests alternative responses.

Check those that apply to you.

( ) When I'm bored, distressed, or pressured, I'm seldom able to think of "something to do" to keep me busy and interested and to take my mind off the problem.

( ) I often find myself apologizing for (and feeling guilty about) my childish reactions and behavior — being rebellious, cranky, sullen, angry, and so on.

( ) At times I would like to follow the rules that I've learned, but my Child is so rebellious (or sullen) that my Adult gives in and the Parent in me feels rejected.

( ) If asked which ego state really controls my personality, I would have to say my Child, not my Adult.

( ) I find I'm constantly blurting out emotional responses — even when they are not called for.

If you checked any of the above, you may want to develop a self-contract to do some self re-Childing.

"Do what I say, not what I do."

"I'll make the decisions in this family."

"If at first you don't succeed, try harder."

"That's the way it's always been done, so do it."

The knowledgeable Adult is responsible for recognizing ego-state imbalances and contaminations. It views the three ego states in perspective and recognizes inappropriate behavior. The Adult sees the need for re-Parenting and, during self-re-Parenting, the Adult substitues for the Parent until the process is complete.

Check those that apply to you.

( ) I frequently find myself unreasonably critical of others.

( ) Even when I don't want to, my overnurturing Parent takes over with others and I ignore myself.

( ) I have a lot of ingrained prejudices that I wish I didn't have, but I can't think of other ways of behaving.

( ) I find myself maneuvering people into situations where they are dependent on me.

( ) If asked which ego state really controls my personality, I would have to say my Parent, not my Adult.

( ) I would like to have more fun, but my Parent is so strongly prohibitive that my Adult gives up and the Child in me feels hopeless.

If you checked any of the above, you may want to develop a self-contract to do some self re-Parenting.

"There's only one right way and that's mine."

"I'm glad I've avoided inheriting my dad's pushiness."

"I still think women are the weaker sex."

"Children should be seen and not heard."

"I don't have to do it like my mother did."

Prejudices learned from parent figures are the most common sources of Adult contamination. The Adult is contaminated when people believe their actions are based on an Adult fact, when actually they are operating under the influence of a Parent prejudice.

Make a list of some of the more obvious prejudices that your parent figures held, e.g., about religion, sexism, lifestyle, and so on.

Prejudices of my parental figures	*I still have it somewhat*	*I got rid of it*
______________________________	( )	( )
______________________________	( )	( )
______________________________	( )	( )
______________________________	( )	( )
______________________________	( )	( )

You might like to self-contract, first,to find out *how* you were able to rid yourself of certain prejudices (education, experience, training, etc.) and,second, to apply the same processes to the Parental prejudices that still contaminate your Adult.

"I'm ugly, ugly, ugly and I always will be."

"If I just wait long enough, he'll come back."

"Poor, dumb, and no good, that's me."

"What if I get sick or lose my job or something."

"I can do anything I want to do — and nothing can stop me."

Unrealistic self-esteem or condemnation — learned or felt — is a common source of Child contamination. For example, people may be convinced that they're dumb (when they're not) or not important (when they are) or not OK (when they can be OK) or better than everybody else (when they're not) or that something magical will happen to transform their lives (when it probably won't), and so on.

Note a few of the unhelpful ways you've learned to think about yourself, that is, some negative or grandiose feelings you may have toward yourself. Then, allow your Adult to suggest alternate helpful ways of feeling for each negative one.

Unhelpful feelings	*Ways I would like to feel*
______________________	______________________
______________________	______________________
______________________	______________________
______________________	______________________

You may like to design a self-contract for bringing your negative feelings more in line with the right-hand column.

"When I'm tempted to get angry, I count to ten."

"When I get depressed, I take out my knitting."

"When I want to strike my kids, I begin vacuuming the floor."

"I scrub floors when I have no answers to life."

There are times when control of the personality is taken over by either Parent or Child. In some cases, even when the Adult observes what's happening, the Adult seems temporarily unable to do anything to change the situation. In other cases, the Adult could avert the situation if it had "something to do." This is a basic TA technique, to give the Adult something to do if the Parent or Child is overactive.

Make a list of things you could do when faced with imminent takeover by Parent or Child. List things that could distract or diffuse an inappropriate response.

My self-controlling skills	*New self-controlling skills I could learn*
______________________	______________________
______________________	______________________
______________________	______________________
______________________	______________________

Keep this list handy in places where personality takeover seems likely.

"I can analyze myself if I find out how."

"I talk more than I listen. I wonder why."

"I want to discover why I'm so scared."

"If I could type better, I'd get a raise."

"I'm going back to school, even if I am 45 years old."

Not all self-contracts have to do with self-therapy and self-repair. You may also contract to use your Adult *to collect data,* e.g., to discover the contents of your Parent ego state, or to find out where your Child responses are strongest. You may also contract to *learn new skills,* e.g., the art of listening, how to express feelings, or rules for macrame.

Note some areas where you need self-contracts that relate to collecting more information about yourself.

New data about myself that I want	*New skills that would interest me*
____________________	____________________
____________________	____________________
____________________	____________________
____________________	____________________

Contracts I could make if I commit myself to discovering the new data and skills: ____________________

____

____

"Sometimes I act as if I have it all together."

"I've got the concern, facts, and feelings to effect the change."

"I'm worried about my neighbor who was jailed. I'm sure he was unjustly accused, so I'm going to get the facts."

Re-Adulting, in the fullest sense of the term, happens only when the three parts of the Adult are clearly recognized .

The warm, sympathetic feelings of the passionate Child, who empathizes with other people's needs and suffering, flow into the *empathetic Adult,* motivating it to do something.

The fair, just, and conscientious Parent, who believes in positive universal values, takes a stand on behalf of others in need, and these values, along with their demand for action, flow into the *ethical Adult.*

The *technical Adult,* fortified with facts and information and moved by the energy flowing from the Parent and Child, examines the alternatives for action and decides how the personality shall act.

Recall a social problem to which you responded with all three parts of your Adult. Describe how your *technical Adult* evaluated the social need, how your *empathetic Adult* grasped the feelings of others in the situation, and how your *ethical Adult* urged you to act.

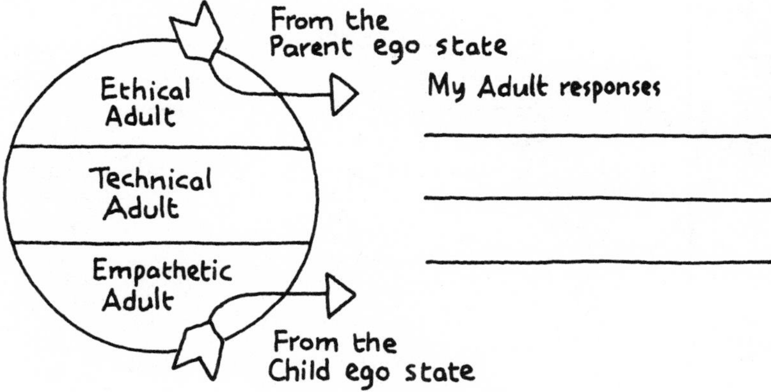

"I'm going to collect contributions for the Cancer Fund."

"I've thought it over, and joining the Peace Corps is what I most want to do."

"I'm starting to study the use of synthetic foods that can supplement diets of starving people."

Integration of the Adult is a large order, only possible because of the inherent power of the inner core with its urge to live and relate to others in a meaningful way. Adult integration always leads to a personal commitment to social values, an identification with others' grief and suffering, and a choosing to do something to improve the world, perhaps even crusading against the universal enemies of human life — war, hunger, disease, and death.

List some of the things you have done that indicate a broader social concern. Which of the universal enemies were involved — war, hunger, disease, or death?

My acts of social concern	*The universal enemy involved*
____________________	____________________
____________________	____________________
____________________	____________________

If this list involves only specific individuals, consider expanding your concern.

Notes

7 Self Re-Parenting

The old and new Parent ego state

All ego states are subject to change. This chapter is about the ways people can change their Parent ego state by a self re-Parenting process. "Self re-Parenting is a procedure for updating and restructuring the Parent ego state. It includes both a theory and a process."[1]

The theory is that the old recordings in the Parent ego state, being historical experiences, cannot be removed or even changed. But through self re-Parenting, the Parent ego state can be restructured. New Parent content can be added, while archaic material can be relegated to a less dominant position. In this way, a New Parent ego state develops which includes both old and new Parenting patterns. According to the theory, each person personally decides what their New Parent will be.

In the process of self re-Parenting, you will first recognize your mother, father, and other parent figures for what they were. Like all parents, they exhibited some behavior that was critical, some that was nurturing, some that was rational, some that was irrational, some that was rebellious, some that was compliant, etc. In a word, all mothers and fathers are less than perfect and need to be forgiven for their inadequacies.

The courage to re-Parent

Self re-Parenting is a courageous act. It starts with the awareness that completely positive parenting was not available in childhood. Because of this experience, the inner Child may hurt or feel cheated, confused, deprived, or angry.

It is easy to put the blame for one's failure to mature on poor parenting. It is easy to say, "It's their fault that I'm critical or rebellious or impulsive, because they never taught me otherwise."

On the other hand, it takes courage to analyze less-than-perfect parent figures and their patterns that are now a part of you. It takes courage to learn new and more effective ways of caring for yourself. Knowing there were OK things about your natural parents accelerates the self re-Parenting process, and enables your Child to give up not-OK feelings toward your natural parents.

In self re-Parenting, you will use your strong new Adult to develop new Parent behavior and messages in order to help balance off negative patterns you may have in your old Parent ego state.

When re-Parenting, you will, in essence, imagine pushing to one side the unwanted patterns of your parent figures (such as your Mom and Dad) that are in your Parent ego state, so that room is made for New Parent content.

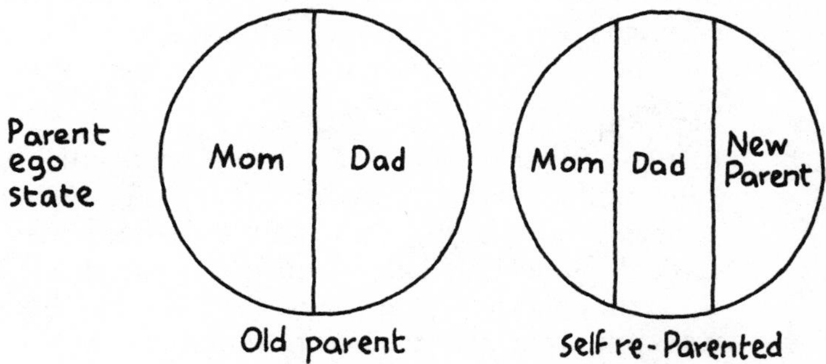

Other Parenting sources

Not everyone has a mother and father in their Parent ego state. People who were taken care of by a grandmother, an aunt, older sibling, and so forth usually incorporate these people into their Parent ego state.

Self re-Parenting is a common process and may continue throughout life. Many people are unaware that they have been self re-Parenting for years — for example, when they incorporate new Parent rules and messages from other significant authorities, perhaps their teachers or school advisors. These other authorities can be positive or negative additions to the parents they originally had.

Clarifying Parental "behavior"

Parental "behavior" — the pointing index finger — is not always an expression of the Parent ego state. Parental behavior may come from any ego state and be uniquely different for different people. Berne clarified this: "The pointed index finger may be a Parental admonition, an Adult indicator, or a Child's accusation."[2] This may be one reason that parenting styles vary with different cultures. People use different ego states to parent.

Frequently, intelligent Parenting comes from the Adult acting either as a substitute parent or as an executive determining when and how behavior from the Parent ego state is appropriate.

The accusation, "You're in your Parent," that some people make when a person points an index finger is simply not universally true. For example, Berne notes that sometimes a therapist, *playing a supportive Parent role,* may really be in the Child ego state, "very much like a little boy playing doctor."[3] A person who has a "short fuse" and explodes easily with children may be parenting with a lot of the Child ego state that is short on patience.

A sign of health

Eric Berne says that the Parent is the weakest member of the personality.[4] However, a healthy Parent ego state is the sign of a healthy personality. People grow mentally healthy when they learn how to Parent well.

Motivation for re-Parenting springs from the inner core, where the urge to live in meaningful ways resides. The ability to carry out a re-Parenting process happens when the Adult can get in touch with these inner-core urges, make life-enhancing self-contracts, and keep them.

Types of parents and children

"I'll kill myself if you do that again."

"My little baby, I don't want you to ever grow up."

"You just wait 'til your father comes home. He'll teach you!"

"There's a place for everything and everything in its place."

Some people's personality problems are due to a faulty Parent ego state. For example, they may have an inadequate, inconsistent Parent, or one that is self-punishing, or one that is physically or verbally destructive of other people.

Here are some typical types of parents. What kind of children might they have as a result of their parenting style?

Type of parent	*Type of child*
Overcritical parent	______________
Overprotective parent	______________
Inconsistent parent	______________
Conflicting parent	______________
Uninvolved parent	______________
Superorganized parent	______________
Emotionally overneedy parent	______________

"Don't bother me with questions."

"I never can decide what to fix the family for dinner."

"We'll do it my way or not at all."

"I can always finish it if you're too tired."

In order to utilize Parent recordings, you will need to become aware of how and when you are presently using inappropriate ones. Many people learn to recognize Parent expressions best by identifying them in others.

Select and observe two people in your own life. Note their Parenting expressions for a period of time, either at work or at home, and observe what message the words they use accompanies.

Parent expressions noticed in others

Words or phrases	*Tone of voice*	*Facial expressions and body language*	*Underlying message*
____________	____________	____________	____________
____________	____________	____________	____________
____________	____________	____________	____________
____________	____________	____________	____________
____________	____________	____________	____________
____________	____________	____________	____________

"I'm glad you were born."

"I enjoy being your dad."

"Let's all go to the ball game together."

"You're a lovely girl and I love you."

Occasionally, people have had such superb parents that they need no re-Parenting. More often, however, people do need a new Parent to supplement the old one. Some need more of a new Parent than others. The first step in discovering how much of a new Parent you need is to identify the most influential parent figures you incorporated into your Parent ego state, for the most part without thinking.

Name the people who most influenced you when you were a young child. Be sure to include your mother and father, older sibling, housekeeper, etc., or whoever acted as a parent when you were young. Below each person's name, list at least five words to describe that person *the way you perceived them when you were a child.*

Sources of my Parent ego state

Name ________	Name ________	Name ________
Words to describe them:	*Words to describe them:*	*Words to describe them:*
____________	____________	____________
____________	____________	____________
____________	____________	____________
____________	____________	____________

"My mother was harsh and domineering, but she did have a good mind."

"My dad was a hard worker, but puritanical."

"My mother would fall apart in crises, but she was very loving."

"My dad liked to watch sports, but was never good at them himself."

Most people, in their Parent ego state, have both *positive* and *negative* qualities. Some qualities are more noticeable than others. Some hinder, some help. If the adjectives on your list for the last exercise were *positive,* you may exhibit these qualities yourself when you act from your Parent ego state. If the adjectives on your lists were *negative,* you may have a tendency to exhibit these qualities yourself when you act from your Parent ego state.

In the left column below list the adjectives from the last exercise that you consider *negative.* In the right column next to each negative adjective, place whatever positive adjective from your list you think might help create a balance.

Negative qualities in my Parent ego state history		*Positive qualities in my Parent ego state history*
________________	is balanced by	________________
________________	is balanced by	________________
________________	is balanced by	________________
________________	is balanced by	________________

"Where will the class for prospective parents be held?"

"What are some good books to read on parenting?"

"See those parents ignoring their toddler by the drain ditch? That's terrible."

"That little girl looks like she needs a doctor. Where are the parents?"

The first step of self re-Parenting is becoming aware of the need; the second step is to analyze the strengths and weaknesses of your historical parents; and the third is to *get education in parenting.* This is a task for the Adult. It requires reading about parent-children relationships and objectively observing their interactions in school, stores, and so forth. Many people assume they know how to be parents just because they are. Yet few people are educated in the basic principles.

Go down to a supermarket at a busy time of day and watch how parents are handling their children. Do the same at a theatre, a drive-in restaurant, and a museum. List what you think was OK and Not-OK parent behavior.

OK parenting	*Not-OK parenting*
____________________	____________________
____________________	____________________
____________________	____________________
____________________	____________________

Contract to read at least one book on the subject of parenting.

"What do you want, honey? What do you need?"

"Is there anything I can do to make you happy?"

"What will help you feel more confident?"

"What can I do so you'll know I love you?"

A dialogue between your Adult ego state and your own inner Child is the next step in self re-Parenting. In the process, your Adult gently questions the Child to determine specific needs you have. Your Child may want holding, or more nutritious food, or more time for relaxation, or more friends, etc.

Get into a quiet, comfortable position and ask your inner Child, "What do you *want?*"
Listen for the answers and fill in the blanks:

__________ __________ __________ __________

Then ask yourself, "What do you *need?*"
Listen for the answers and fill in the blanks:

__________ __________ __________ __________

Now look at your wants and needs. Are they similar or different? In what ways?

Let your Adult, like a healthy Parent, think about your Child's needs and desires.

"I'm going to plan for a fun party."

"What will I need to do differently to find time to paint?"

"Yes, I do need to get some nurturing friends."

"It's not bad to laugh hard and loud, so I will."

"I can't have it now, but maybe at a later date."

Some people who know what their Child wants or needs allow their inner Parent to dominate with "yes" or "no" answers. Others use their Adult to evaluate the requests and say "yes," unless there is a major reason for saying "no." If the Child wants the impossible dream, then a "no" is appropriate. If a possible substitute replaces the impossible dream, it comforts the Child.

List your Child's requests, then the information you already have or need to get before deciding "yes" or "no."

My Child's requests	*Pertinent data needed before I decide*
____________________	____________________
____________________	____________________
____________________	____________________
____________________	____________________
____________________	____________________

"Of course you'd like a trip to Europe. Now, how might I start to plan it?"

"Naturally you want to feel safer. I'll get new locks for the door."

"Everyone needs some time for themselves. Take one hour a day to enjoy relaxing."

"It's OK to want to get ahead. Start with an inexpensive night-school class."

During this step of self re-Parenting, the Adult ego state takes on a new task. It acts as a referee, *protects* the Child from negative inner dialogue from the old Parent, and *substitutes* as a positive new Parent until the new Parent is established. It makes rational responses to the Child's requests.

Make a list of things your inner Child felt like doing this week. Note your responses to your Child feelings. Then, guess from which ego state your response came — Parent, Adult, or Child.

Things my Child wanted	*How I responded to my Child*	*Ego state that seemed to respond*

"I will continue taking care of my Child."

"I like the changes I am making."

"I need to keep aware of my old useless habits."

"New skills don't come easily; I'll be patient with myself."

"My Child doesn't have to be perfect, nor my Adult and Parent."

During the weeks and months that the Adult acts as a healthy substitute parent, it needs to make and keep contracts. These protect the Child. They also give permission to the Child to redecide early negative decisions, experiment, and practice new Child behavior. At the same time, the Adult is practicing new parenting behavior. At last the day comes when the *new parenting is automatic* rather than continuously planned and thought out by the Adult. When automatic, it has become part of the new Parent ego state. The child has nothing to fear. A new self is well on its way.

Complete the columns below.

Permissions for my Child	*Adult contracts needed*
______________________	______________________
______________________	______________________
______________________	______________________
______________________	______________________
______________________	______________________

"I like taking care of kids."

"I thought it would be fun to have a baby, but it's just one diaper after another."

All parent figures, being persons, have three ego states. If you were reared by a mother and a father, your Parent ego state would be like this:

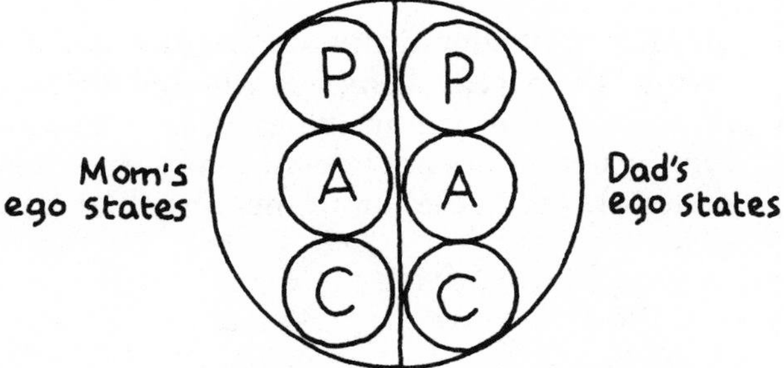

If you were cared for by others, they would be in your Parent. Some people use parenting behavior from the Parent ego state. Sometimes, it comes from the Child, as though playing house, or from the Adult who thinks about parenting, then acts better than the natural parents once acted.

List some common behaviors or statements your parent figures used. After each, guess what ego state it came from and label it P, A, or C.

Parent-figure behavior or statements	*Ego state*
______________________________	______
______________________________	______
______________________________	______

Understanding, then forgiving

"I'll bet mom's mother was even more prejudiced than mom is."

"Dad was labeled 'useless' when he was a kid."

"Mom has passed on to me the habit of punishing she learned as a child."

"When I see Grandpa lose control, I realize where my temper tantrums come from."

An important step in any re-Parenting activity involves "forgiving" the parenting figures who instilled the unwanted Parent material in you in the first place. In most cases, the parenting figures are not to blame, for, very often, the unwanted material was passed on to them by their parenting figures.

In a quiet moment, allow yourself to relax, and go back in time to when your parenting figures were little children. Imagine them being trained by their own parents. See them learning the negative characteristics they later exhibited as parents. Allow yourself to experience how they felt, how they reacted, and how they learned this response, probably without thinking. Fully entering a fantasy like this will allow you to see your unwanted Parent material in a broader perspective.

Record some of your reactions to your fantasy ___________

____

The fantasy experience may make it easier for you to "forgive" your parents and appreciate them. They probably did the best they knew how to do.

"My parents were pioneers in their way."

"My father lived only to make money."

"Doing things for people in need was my mother's way of life."

"My parents once believed only in saying 'no,' but now they often say 'yes'."

The way people use their Parent ego state is often influenced by the meaning and value they give to their life. Also, people connect their life meaning to the ways they behave; consequently, they fear that changing their behavior and attitudes in any way may force them to change their life meaning, which most people are reluctant to do.

In your opinion, what were your parents' pervasive meanings in life? What did they live for? What were their most important values? ______________________________

____

Did your parents ever change their life meanings in any way?

In what ways? ______________________________

____

What of your parents' life-meaning have you incorporated into your own life? ______________________________

8 Self Re-Childing

The Child misvalued

In an overeager desire to be fully human, to find meaning and purpose in life, and to serve the community and the world, some people misvalue the Child ego state in themselves and others. They may underrate it or overrate it.

For example, it is not uncommon for well-meaning people, dedicated to helping others, to *undervalue* and restrict their own Child ego states. The Child in such "helpful" people may suffer from unfulfilled essential needs — the need to play, to be spontaneous, to express positive emotions like joy and love, to express negative feelings like anger and fear. Such people may be cold and critical toward themselves and place a low value on their own feelings, while remaining sympathetic to the feelings of others.

Others misvalue the Child ego state by *overvaluing* it. In such people, often described as immature, the Child is predominant and frequently out of control. Fully occupied with their own feelings, desires, wishes, and dreams, they tend to live almost always on an emotional level. Even when a rational response is explicitly asked for, they respond only with feelings — usually negative ones, like anxiety, resentment, or rejection.

Whenever the Child ego state is misvalued — either underrated or overrated — re-Childing is in order.

The Child is an important part of the personality and an important source of power. Its OKness is crucial in developing a new self. Most people are capable of exhibiting an exciting and vivacious personality when the Child ego state feels OK.

With a healthy Child ego state, a person can be an attractive, sensitive, spontaneous, warm, affectionate, fun-loving, outgoing, and creative person. These are some of the positive qualities that can be traced to a healthy, happy Child. Such qualities can be a strong asset to a committed person who, for example, wants to spread enthusiasm for a project, or to a hardworking person who wants to relax during periods of stress and pressure.

The three-part Child

While reading this chapter, remember your Child ego state is the child you once were. Some of it you may have already modified. Other portions may need to be changed in order to enhance your life.

The objective of re-Childing is to create a balanced personality *between* the three ego states and *within* the Child ego state, so that in the total personality each part of the Child can be used appropriately.

Self re-Childing can be done best when the three parts of the Child are understood and their manners of response are identified.

The *Natural Child* is the impulsive infant in all of us that seeks comfort and struggles to avoid pain. It wants to eat when it wants to eat, sleep when it wants to sleep, and so forth. The *Little Professor* is the intuitive and creative part of the personality that strives to manipulate its environment to meet the needs of the Natural Child. By trial and error it learns how to cry to get mother's attention. Next is the *Adapted Child,* the part of the Child that responds to training, traumas, and daily experiences. Children are trained to adapt to others' expectations soon after birth.

The most common *responses* of an Adapted Child to training are rebellion, compliance, and procrastination. These responses are survival techniques. The Little Professor experiments with them until discovering what works best in a given situation.

Graphically, the Child ego state is made up of the Adapted Child, the Little Professor, and the Natural Child.

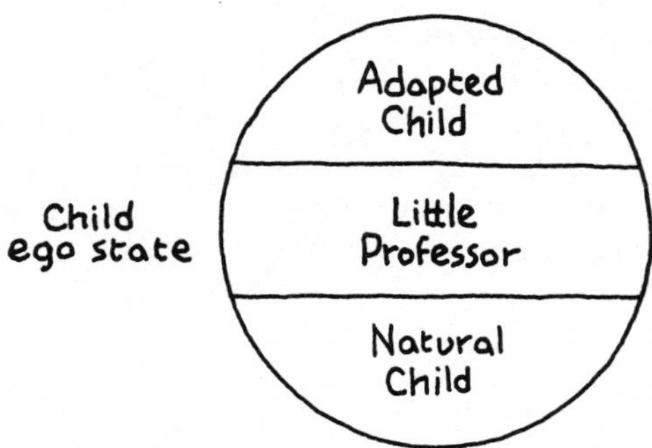

A creative act

Self re-Childing is a creative act. It releases an uncensored part of the Child (Natural Child) that has the urge to be free. It releases an intuitive part of the Child (Little Professor) that has the urge to relate to others. And, it releases an OK conditioned part of the Child (Adapted Child) that has the urge to experience its own potential and the potential of its environment.

Releasing your Child is a growth process, a lifelong process that can add new meaning to your existence and to the experience of your new self.

"I give up. Nothing has meaning anymore."

"Day after day I find myself doing stupid things."

"Why shouldn't I get angry!"

"I'm afraid to say what I think."

Many people need practice in recognizing responses that come from their Child ego states, especially those that are negative and self-defeating. Your Child can feel not-OK without your Adult realizing it. One of the stages in self re-Childing is learning to recognize your not-OK Child in action.

Following is a list of common negative Child responses. Check those that you recognize.

	That's often me	*That's me sometimes*	*That's not me*
I put things off and then I feel guilty about it.	( )	( )	( )
I play stupid, even when I really know what's going on.	( )	( )	( )
I sulk when I don't get my way.	( )	( )	( )
I'm mad if things don't go my way.	( )	( )	( )
When I want a rest, I tense up and feel I don't deserve it.	( )	( )	( )
I find that I can't say "no" to people.	( )	( )	( )
I am afraid to say anything negative, even if it's true.	( )	( )	( )

"People enjoy themselves with me."

"I'm excited over my new positive feelings."

"Making changes takes guts, and I've got guts."

"I'm glad I can show my wife how much I love her."

Some people believe they make few OK-Child responses. In reality, their Child responses may be very subtle or overadapted — like children who act like grown-ups. Such people are often unaware of their OK-Child responses.

To get in touch with more of your OK Child, list some of the events, people, and experiences that you find:

Exciting and challenging

____

____

Warm and affectionate

____

____

Funny and laughable

____

____

Restful and relaxing

____

____

Energizing and activating

____

____

____

"I always ran and hid when my father came home."

"My mother was easy to psych out."

"Eating is what I liked best."

Being afraid of parents or other powerful people is a common experience for many children. They may adapt or adjust to the powerful person's demands, or they may fight rebelliously against them (Adapted Child). In many cases, the choice of flight or fight is a Child's intuitive, creative decision made by picking up the "vibrations" in the situation and "psyching out" what they mean in terms of rewards and punishments (Little Professor). Children, like grownups, live in their bodies and seek a pleasant, relaxed state of homeostasis (Natural Child).

Write a few lines about some emotional experience that happened to you when you were little.

____

____

____

Did you respond (NC) like it was a fight for survival or a pleasurable physical experience? ____________

Did you respond intuitively and creatively (LP) to manipulate the situation? ____________

Did you respond as you were taught to do (AC), as you were conditioned? ____________

"Waa waa, mmm mm."

"It tastes good."

"My tummy hurts."

"Get away."

The Natural Child is what a baby would be "naturally" if nothing or no one influenced it to be otherwise. It is the untrained, uncensored expressive infant within. It is naturally centered on itself, concerned only with its own feelings, satisfaction, and pleasure.

The Natural Child is capable of violence, like throwing a baby bottle out of a crib, and of delight, like splashing when playing in a tub of water. However, its responses are amoral. It is not concerned with good or bad, but simply follows its impulsive desires.

What are some experiences (positive or negative) that you remember expressing through your Natural Child when you were little?

Positive experiences and responses	*Negative experiences and responses*
______________________	______________________
______________________	______________________
______________________	______________________
______________________	______________________
______________________	______________________

"I want what I want and I want it now."

"Rub my back."

"Give me something to eat."

"I want to go swimming."

"I'm sleepy."

"Wow, I feel alive."

"If I don't get some water, I feel I might faint."

Throughout life, the Natural Child is centered around bodily needs. If needs are not met, people may regress into excessive sleep, or become ill, or die. If they *are* met, people are energized. A consistently happy person usually indicates a healthy Natural Child. Your Natural Child allows you to respond spontaneously to rhythm, melody, colors, scents, tastes, joys, and bodily pleasures. It responds to bodily feelings — like a good meal, dancing, sexual experiences, exercises, etc.

Check out your Natural Child responses.

Responses	*That's seldom me*	*That's sometimes me*	*That's often me*
I enjoy eating.	( )	( )	( )
I sleep easily and deeply.	( )	( )	( )
My body feels good to me.	( )	( )	( )
I like sun on my skin.	( )	( )	( )
Being in the water feels exhilarating.	( )	( )	( )
I enjoy responding sexually.	( )	( )	( )
I like listening to music.	( )	( )	( )
The beat of drums gets to me.	( )	( )	( )

	That's seldom me	*That's some-times me*	*That's often me*
Hearing wind in the trees is my thing.	( )	( )	( )
I like the crash of ocean waves.	( )	( )	( )
The taste of strawberries is sweet to me.	( )	( )	( )
Warm milk toast soothes me.	( )	( )	( )
Daphne in the spring has meaning to me.	( )	( )	( )
I like the smell of hickory smoke.	( )	( )	( )
Feeling sand between my toes is great.	( )	( )	( )
The smell of the earth in the spring is it.	( )	( )	( )
The sight of the first snowfall thrills me.	( )	( )	( )
Shadows on a granite cliff . . .	( )	( )	( )
Smiles on peoples' faces . . .	( )	( )	( )
Soft touch from others . . .	( )	( )	( )
Holding when I'm tired . . .	( )	( )	( )

Now make your list — all the things that appeal to each one of your senses.

"I've got a hunch."

"I think I'll experiment and see what happens."

"Let me see if I can figure it out."

"We're on the same wavelength."

The Little Professor is the emerging Adult in the Child. Often, young children who have not developed their own knowledge and experience demonstrate a sort of primitive wisdom. They intuit what's going on inside other people. They create new roles, objects, and situations for themselves. They manipulate people and things to get what they want. They often play their hunches. They are creative.

List examples of Little Professor activity that you recall from childhood. Find examples from home and school, when playing, eating, relating, "surviving," etc.

If you discover that many of your Little Professor activities were not-OK manipulative, you may choose to make a self re-Childing contract around these areas.

"I've got another hunch."

"I can guess what she's feeling."

"I'll bet I can figure that out."

"I'll try other ways to make it work."

With a little jogging of the memory, most people can easily identify their Little Professor hard at work all during childhood.

Too often in adult life, this irreplaceable font of ideas and creative responses is forgotten, or at least underestimated. Too often, people turn off their intuitive abilities and consequently may not be aware of their inner-core urges.

Locate situations in your life now where you have used or still use your Little Professor. Consider work, home, school, activities, hobbies, friendships, free time, and so on.

______________________	______________________
______________________	______________________
______________________	______________________
______________________	______________________
______________________	______________________

If you find little to note here, it may indicate that your Little Professor has been overly restricted. Perhaps you need to "tune in" by using your intuition more.

"Don't you ever, ever talk back to me again!"

"Your brother was just hit by a car."

"Wash your hands and comb your hair."

"You'll have to do your homework before you play."

All children adapt to the things they experience and the words they hear. Some adaptations are useful throughout life; others are useless or destructive. Most people have both kinds of adaptations. Discovering what they are is part of re-Childing. The negative ones can then be replaced and positive ones can be learned.

List some important events that happened to you in childhood, also some specific training your parents insisted on. What responses did your Child make that led to later adaptations? For example, if parents are overdemanding, children often respond with, "In a minute," or "After a while," etc. This becomes a procrastinating adaptation pattern.

Events and training	*Responses and adaptations*

"I wouldn't dare do that."

"I like to look nice before I go out."

"If people don't like the way I talk, who cares."

"I feel so strange in new situations that I seldom go out socially."

Adaptations in childhood — for better and worse — continue to strongly control people's personalities. Feelings of guilt, inadequacy, success, and competence often come from this source, as does the script. For example, some people continually want others' approval and act out drama parts and repeat expected lines to get this approval. Some continually expect disapproval (because they got it when they were little) and act in ways to get it.

List some of your childhood adaptations, such as being polite or fearful, which are experienced in your curent life. Check those that need to be replaced with more satisfying ones, and if so, in what way. Be specific.

Childhood adaptations	*OK or not OK*	*Not-OK adaptations to be replaced with*

"It's not necessary to explode in anger just because I always have."

"The Adult truth is, I'm competent, not incompetent — regardless of how my Child feels."

"I don't need to be lonely anymore. I can find new friends."

Re-Childing involves the cooperation of your Natural Child and your Little Professor with your Adult and positive parts of your Parent.

The Little Professor unknowingly tries to solve inner conflict, especially if the Natural Child wants something that the Adapted Child has been taught is a "no-no." Here the Adult and Parent ego states need to be consciously co-opted and used.

To use your three-part Child more freely, list some bodily pleasures you wanted this week and indicate the way you responded to these desires.

Bodily feelings and desires (NC)	*What I was conditioned to do with these kinds of feelings (AC)*	*My hunch about what I should do (LP)*	*What my Adult and OK Parent need to do to help*
____________	____________	____________	____________
____________	____________	____________	____________
____________	____________	____________	____________

Now list some other kinds of things you wanted to do in order to express yourself creatively, and go through the same process of analysis.

"It doesn't mean anything to me when I'm so tired."

"I can guess what it means. Figuring out things is fun."

"I really like getting approval for what I do."

The Adapted Child often finds meaning when experiencing self-esteem or receiving esteem from others. In fact, a great deal of everyone's behavior is related to their esteem needs.

The Little Professor, also in search of meaning, creatively seeks out others and often intuitively solves problems. In fact, a person may go to sleep with a troublesome unsolved problem and wake up with the answer, because the Little Professor has been working overtime.

The Natural Child, being bodily centered, affects the entire personality. In fact, when people are sick or very tired or hungry, some areas of their life may seem meaningless to them at that time.

For each part of the Child ego state, list ways you currently find meaning.

Adapted Child	*Little Professor*	*Natural Child*
________________	________________	________________
________________	________________	________________
________________	________________	________________

If any part of your Child is not finding meaning, you will need to do more work on your new self.

9 Self Rescripting

Multiple scripts

Most people have more than one script. Scripts may be found in all three ego states. Although the scripts and subscripts in the Child ego state are usually the easiest to identify, we believe, as a result of our personal research, that scripts also originate in the Parent and Adult ego states.

In whatever ego state they occur, scripts are usually played out without awareness of the scripted behavior that is involved.

Scripts in the Child ego state are related to childhood experiences and to the resulting life decisions made at that time. The individual psychological Child scripts are usually expressed in forms such as: "This is the way I was taught to live"; or, "This is the way I choose to live"; or, "This is the way I had to live to survive or get approval." Scripts in the Child ego state include all the script directives learned in childhood. Such directives, given by parent figures, peers, and so forth, were responded to in childhood by compliance or rebellion. But whether or not a person currently complies to the directions given years ago in childhood, his or her Child scripts are present and having their effects.

Scripts in the Parent ego state are often revealed in cultural, religious, national, and family customs, and are usually expressed as, "This is the way things should (or should not) be." Such scripts are incorporated by children into their developing Parent ego states. When you incorporated your parent figures into your Parent ego state, you incorporated all three of their ego states, *including their scripts.* So, in *your* Parent ego state are found directives for the scripts played out by your mother, father, and other parenting figures. People who are constantly in their Parent ego state tend to play out their parents' scripts.

Scripts in the Adult usually refer to general skills, and may be expressed in the form, "This is the way to live effectively and efficiently." These scripts are *technical know-hows.* Although in many cases it is difficult to distinguish Adult know-how from skills in the Parent and Child ego states, a simple test can distinguish *normal* Adult activity from Adult *scripted* behavior. The normal Adult ego state processes here-and-now data and makes decisions based on that data. When following an Adult script, however, the person is acting, certainly with technical skill, but with out-of-date information and by repeating out-of-date decisions. For example, learning to drive a car is an Adult activity. However, although much new information about safe driving has been collected in recent years, many people choose to continue driving with only their out-of-date information — i.e., their Adult scripted behavior.

The need for rescripting

Although many scripts are banal, and many are unhealthy and destructive, some scripts are OK. When people *act* competently and well, and *feel* competent and well, they are not in destructive or going-nowhere scripts. They are either in constructive Parent, Adult, or Child scripts or are using an integrated Adult ego state. They do not need rescripting. Such people are few and far between. Most people need at least a partial rescripting.

When to rescript

The Parent, Adult, and Child ego states can all be rescripted. Some people function primarily from the Parent ego state, and thus repeat the scripts of their parents. With awareness and motivation, the not-OK parts of the Parent ego-state script may be changed by re-Parenting. When people re-Parent themselves, the new Parent that they construct is healthy with a healthy new script, and therefore encourages rewriting of a healthy new Child script.

People who act *constantly* in the Child ego state are almost surely living out emotionally overwhelming Child scripts, which usually exclude rational Adult activity and the nurturing of an OK-Parent ego state. The first, and most difficult, step in Child rescripting is for people to become aware that they are, in fact, in a Child script that contaminates their Adult.

People who function constantly from an objective, technical Adult ego state need rescripting too. Such people have usually been conditioned to "turn off" their nurturing Parent and Fun Child. They get little joy out of life and give little joy to others. They need to develop a more permeable Adult boundary, get in touch with the Child and Parent scripting they already have, and change what needs to be changed. Staying in the Adult all the time is not a TA goal. Instead, the goal is to use all the OK capacities of each ego state. To do this, the Adult needs to become integrated.

When people go through the process of re-Adulting they become more integrated, utilizing OK parts of the Child and Parent scripts and recognizing what still needs to be controlled and changed.

Script free or rescripting

Some people may wonder if it's possible to be script free and totally autonomous. We don't know, as we have never met a person entirely script free. It seems possible that people could be script free temporarily in some part of their ego states. For example, while people are in the Natural Child, *at that time* they would not be into a script.

To us it does not seem necessary for a person to be script free. Rather, it seems more effective and efficient to identify both constructive and destructive script elements and to change those parts that interfere with the development of a new self.

It *is* possible to bring down the curtain on a destructive, or going-nowhere, drama and to *change the balance of the show* so that problems are resolved and the show ends with happy players and an applauding audience.[1] This is rescripting.

If a script is positively rewritten, any player may move into it with the comfortable expectation that everything is going to turn out all right, that meaning will be found because courage and motivation will be high, and the urge to live will be experienced as a powerful inner force.

"My folks enjoyed working together."

"Mom always tried to rescue people."

"Dad was depressed until the end."

"Grandma and Grandpa always worked hard."

Your own parents and parent substitutes were naturally scripted when they were little by the things that happened to them. Like you, their childhood experiences led them to decisions and psychological positions that were played out in later life. Their scripts also had drama *themes* that were observable in the directing of characters in the daily "scenes" and the major "acts" of their lives.

If your parents are dead, they either did or didn't find meaning in this life. If your parents are still alive, they are moving toward the inevitable final curtain. Perhaps they have found significant meaning in a constructive, winning script. Perhaps their scripts are banal and their lives unfulfilling. Perhaps they were scripted in childhood in destructive ways, so that they feel like losers and see life as meaningless.

Recall or observe the patterns of your parents' lives to see if you are living by their scripts.

My parent figures	*Scenes they often played*	*Possible meaning of scenes for them*
________________	________________	________________
________________	________________	________________
________________	________________	________________

OK and Not-OK ways I've copied my parents' acts ________________

"I made many mistakes, son, but I did the best I knew how to do."

"I'm glad I handled my responsibilities as I did."

"Lots of times it was great fun having you kids around."

Many children seem to want more from their parents than their parents are able to give. Because they don't get what they want, children often become resentful and stay resentful for many years. Even as grownups, they may hang onto their anger or depression, unhappy because their parents weren't different. In effect, they ignore the OK parts of their parents and the OK parts of their parents' scripts.

Sit down comfortably and imagine each one of your parents reviewing their own lives.

What might they say about themselves? ________________

____

What roles might they see themselves as having played?

____

What might they express pleasure, even pride for? _______

____

What OK elements in their scripts have you kept for yourself?

____

Dialogue with positive parents

"Dad, do you have something to tell me that you've never told me before?"

"I wish I had taken you to a ball game when you were little."

"Mom, if the past could be done over, what things would you do differently?"

"I wish I had spent more time just *being* with you, not just *doing* for you."

Most people talk to themselves from time to time. They may criticize or compliment themselves or others, argue internally after something has occurred, or rehearse internally before a coming event. Many people are only partially aware of having this habit. Therefore, they may not use it productively.

Learning how to dialogue with the *positive* parts of the parents you once had is an important skill that will accelerate your rescripting.

Sit comfortably in a chair. Put another chair opposite you and imagine one of your parents sitting there. Next, imagine talking to the positive part of your parent, the part that actually wanted (or wants) the best for you because he or she loves you — though the love may not have been expressed often enough or in healthy ways. Imagine also that your parent has grown in wisdom and has some useful advice to give you on how to change something so that your script can be rewritten. Move back and forth between the two chairs during the dialogue. When it feels finished, start a new dialogue with each of your other parent figures. If you have re-Parented yourself, also speak to your new Parent.

When you finish, write down their words of wisdom or their useful advice to you.

"When I was a youngster, I learned how to fix cars and I'm still good at repairing things."

" 'Here's how to do it' is an expression I heard alot."

"I was encouraged to figure things out."

"I do not act impulsively on important issues. I think things out first."

It seems as though many people have scripts in their Adult ego states. These scripts or life plans are technical or intellectual skills that were taught by parents who treated their children intelligently and showed them how to think and do things. If these skills are used automatically they are scripts. Rescripting the Adult involves updating and reevaluating the technical and intellectual skills learned in childhood.

Think of your Adult and the many ways you use it, both automatically in a script way and thoughtfully in a nonscript way.

Technical Adult skills I use automatically	*Skills I use thoughtfully which are not scripted*
________________	________________
________________	________________
________________	________________
________________	________________
________________	________________

"The truth is, I don't have enough facts to go on."

"I need to analyze how to do it."

"I've looked at the problem from every angle and, at last, have all the data."

Solid technical knowledge about yourself and about the way the world is is available from your Adult ego state, but there are also some gaps in your knowledge. After all, both you and the world are continually in a state of change. New challenges arise and new discoveries are made that invalidate old beliefs and ways of doing things. People who are authentic recognize the continuing need for change and for updating information.

First, select a problem you would like to solve. Then, using the double-chair technique, put your well-informed Adult in one chair and your uninformed, misinformed, or partially informed Adult in the other.

Then, start a dialogue with the words, "I have this problem I want to solve which is . . . . What kind of thinking do I need to do or what information do I need to get?" Then from the chair of your well-informed Adult, who is somewhat like a research librarian, begin to express various options. Continue the dialogue as long as authentic possibilities are being discussed.

"I was taught to be competitive and also to play fair."

"As a girl, I was always in the kitchen — and I still am!"

"I was always told, 'Go outside to play,' and I still do."

"I never have any fun inside at home."

The experiences children have, including the injunctions they receive verbally or nonverbally, are like brief scenes in a drama. When these scenes are repetitive or of major significance, they determine the script, the roles that are taken in the script, and the dialogue and action that accompany the roles.

These familiar scenes are often replayed in later life when the Adult is contaminated by the Adapted Child, or when the person functions primarily from the Adapted Child who originally "wrote" the psychological childhood script.

Recall some significant scenes you experienced when you were little and how other people acted with you. Consider whether or not something similar happens to you currently.

Scenes I experienced in childhood	*Other people in the scenes*	*Similar behavior and scenes in my current life*
________________	________________	________________
________________	________________	________________
________________	________________	________________

"Don't bother me, I'm busy."

"Don't act like a baby. Grow up."

"Think about it, you can do it."

"You're wonderful just the way you are."

Many children pick up *positive* scripting messages from their parents. These messages, given verbally or nonverbally, are messages to think, to feel, to be healthy, to be close to others, to succeed, to rejoice. Children with these kinds of messages may not need to rewrite much of their scripts.

Other children get *negative* messages which are often prohibitive injunctions. Common ones are: "Don't be," "Don't be you," "Don't be a child," "Don't be grownup," "Don't be close," "Don't," "Don't make it," "Don't be sane," "Don't be important," "Don't belong."[2]

Most children get a mixture of positive and negative messages. The positive ones need to be deliberately used, the negative ones need to be rewritten.

Check any negative injunctions you received. Record what the positive opposite — a "do permission" — would be. You will need it for your new script. Also record the positive permissions you received as a child. You may need to emphasize them and use them more often in your new script.

Negative injunctions	*Rescripting needed to change the injunctions*
__ Don't be	______________________
__ Don't be you	______________________
__ Don't be a child	______________________

Don't and do injunctions (continued)

Negative injunctions	*Rescripting needed to change the injunctions*
__ Don't grow up	______________
__ Don't be close	______________
__ Don't make it	______________
__ Don't be sane	______________
__ Don't be important	______________
__ Don't belong	______________
__ Don't	______________

Positive "do permissions"	*Rescripting needed to emphasize my permissions*
______________	______________
______________	______________
______________	______________
______________	______________
______________	______________
______________	______________
______________	______________
______________	______________
______________	______________
______________	______________

"I feel absolutely *driven* to be strong and never show my feelings."

"I feel as if I *have* to be perfect."

"For me, it's *essential* that I please others."

"I'm always *hurrying* and *trying* hard, no matter what."

A miniscript is "a sequence of behavior occurring in the matter of minutes or even seconds, that results in a reinforcement pattern for life."[3] Not-OK miniscripts are based on strong parental messages called *drivers*. These seem to be helpful, but actually are burdens, because people who have them believe they are OK *only* if they comply to one or more of the five drivers — being perfect, trying hard, hurrying, pleasing people, or being strong.

Check the drivers you received as a child and how you use them in your current life.

Drivers	*Where and how I use the drivers*
( ) Be strong.	____________________
( ) Be perfect.	____________________
( ) Hurry up.	____________________
( ) Try hard.	____________________
( ) Please others.	____________________

The opposite of drivers are *allowers.* Allowers are permissions to take care of yourself, to be autonomous, to be human. In rescripting your new self you may need to modify your drivers so that they become allowers. What do you need?

Allowers	*Where and how I use the allowers*
( ) It's OK to be open and trust.	______________
( ) It's OK to make mistakes.	______________
( ) It's OK to take your time.	______________
( ) It's OK to do things, not just try to do them.	______________
( ) It's OK to please yourself.	______________

Dialogue with playful Child

"All work and no play has made me a dull boy."

"I read that self-actualizing people enjoy play."

"I agree, I seem to be more effective if I play a bit."

"Being creative is like play to me."

The Natural Child and the Little Professor in each person can be compared to a playful child. A child enjoys and plays with its body and its environment. It responds to positive stimuli with smiles, coos, and gurgles of joy. Children are often taught to deny this universal self and the urge to live a meaningful life. They are adapted to less positive goals and life styles. Playfulness often releases the shackles on the Child so it can recover its basic humanness.

Select a part of your childhood script that needs changing. Use the double-chair technique again. In one chair, imagine you in your old Child ego state — the way you used to be before you started to design a new self. In the other chair, see the Child you are becoming, the one you are rescripting to be — more alive, lovable, loving, creative, and playful.

Start a dialogue between these two "Childs." Let some joy and laughter emerge. Children are essentially playful. Let your new self be that way.

If this seems too difficult, experiment with making silly faces at yourself in a mirror. Someone once said, "People don't stop playing because they're getting old, they get old because they stop playing."

"I like my looks, I need to stop putting myself down."

"Just because I work well doesn't mean I need to work all the time."

"I'm often short tempered at home, never at the office."

All people have some positive qualities. These may be related to their bodily health or appearance; their psychological health, physical behavior, or use of their ego states; or their awareness and use of their inner-core urges and energies.

Most people also would like to change some things about themselves. Selecting these things is the first step in preparing to rewrite a script.

Look over the information you have gathered in this chapter, and in the earlier chapters, "All The World's a Stage" and "Scripts People Play." Then, fill in the following:

Things I like about my scripts	*Things I don't like about my scripts*
______________________	______________________
______________________	______________________
______________________	______________________
______________________	______________________
______________________	______________________
______________________	______________________

Rewriting the last scene

"He was so healthy. How could he die so suddenly with a heart attack?"

"He just plain drank himself to death."

"She showed everybody how to live in the pain she suffered when dying."

"One night he looked very tired, just smiled at us, went to bed, and never woke up."

The final curtain falls for many people in unexpected ways and when they are least prepared for it. For others, it seems inevitable because of their scripting behavior. A few people, because of their pain and suffering, welcome the end of their life dramas.

In any case, the final scene is inevitably played out and the curtain must fall. The last scene may be superb and the "audience" appreciative, or it may be dismal and the audience merely indifferent. Often the choice is yours.

Imagine the time you have left to live is limited. What might you still want to do?

If I had only ten years left to live I would ____________

If I had only one year left to live I would ____________

If I had only a month left to live I would ____________

If I had only a day left to live I would ____________

The meaning this reflects in my life is ____________

"Now that I know what to change about me, I need to decide how to do it."

"Slimming down will require a strong contract."

"More flexibility with problems is what I need."

"I never before realized I had inner power."

To become aware of both positive and negative qualities in oneself is a courageous act. The motivation for it is stimulated by the inner core's urge to live — to be free, to relate to others, to experience and analyze, to make and carry out decisions. The plans for change are the contracts that are required.

List something you want to change about yourself *now*. Design the contract that would be necessary.

I could change ____________ about myself and do __________

______________ instead of ____________________ which I now do.

By making this change, my script would also change and the

next act would be ______________________________________

Therefore, I will contract to ______________________________

If this works for you, use the same technique for something else you want to change.

10 Releasing the Inner Core

Energies and the inner core

Deep inside each person is an inner core, a wellspring of life that wants to burst forth and express itself. It is an energy source that gives life to each of the three ego states and unifies them.

Each ego state is unique and each has value. You have discovered some of these values. You have also learned that some people have rigid ego state boundaries and, consequently, their energy does not flow easily among their ego states. Most people experience some fogged thinking in the Adult, as childhood conditioning and childlike feelings leak through the ego state boundary and contaminate clear Adult thinking. So, too, with parental opinions, prejudices, and traditions. Few people are aware of their contaminators. They like to think of themselves as Adult, even when they aren't.

Your inner core, where the deepest sense of self is experienced, is the plus part of your personality. When you are open to this inner core, you feel creative and alive, courageous and motivated, able to solve problems, able to enjoy yourself and others more and more.

But sometimes the inner core is closed and blocked. When this happens, people use expressions like: "I lack willpower"; or, "My energies are rapidly drained"; or, "My hidden potential seems to stay hidden"; or, "I wish I could work at full capacity"; or, "Trying to improve is simply exhausting." These statements imply that, in addition to possible ego state problems, the person's inner core does not seem to be freely flowing and energizing the personality.

A person's own vitality, the source of his or her own inner forces, can sometimes, unfortunately, be deflected from its constructive goal of health and fulfillment and used instead in the service of sickness and destructiveness.

Getting in touch with your inner core

This chapter suggests ways for you to get in touch with your source of inner-core energy and to explore ways of releasing personal potential.

As Eric Berne wrote:

> Each person designs his own life. Freedom gives him the power to carry out his own designs, and power gives him the freedom to interfere with the designs of others. Even if the outcome is decided by men he has never met or germs he will never see, his last words and the words on his gravestone will cry out his striving.[1]

While the self has freedom energy to carry out its own designs and to support the designs of others, the self may also block its own designs and interfere with those of others.

The urge to live

Yet, even in the midst of blocking its own capacities, the self seems to experience the "urge to live." This inner movement is felt as an inextinguishable power within. Sometimes this power expresses itself as a voice — not the voice of your historical parents or of the child you once were, but an energizing voice speaking from the deepest part of you, calling you to ever fuller life.

The four expressions of the urge to live — the urge to be free, to relate to others, to experience and analyze, and to make and carry out decisions — are common to all selves.

The urge to live, the most basic urge, is a universal, not a unique, characteristic. If the urge to live is diminished, as it sometimes is with suffering, energy drops rapidly and the person may no longer be energized to be free, to relate to others, to experience and analyze, and to make and carry out decisions. These things lose their meaning. If you lose the urge to live from time to time, it is a sign that your inner core is in some way restricted.

Releasing the inner core — the process explored in this chapter — helps you to be who you are and use what you have to use, in yourself and in your environment, to recover the sense of meaning and the joy of your new self.

You can get in touch with your power. Thus, throughout life, you can develop an ever-new new self. A self so empowered works harmoniously and effectively on all levels of being — the biological self, the psychological self, and the self of the inner core.

"I could kill him, the way I feel."

"One thing I know about myself is I'm responsible."

"I don't like gossiping and I don't do it."

"I could cheat a bit and get away with it."

Exploring the inner core involves a willingness to plumb beneath the surface of ego-state responses. For some, coming to acknowledge the possibilities of good as well as destructiveness in themselves seems threatening. But an honest awareness and acceptance of our potential (positive and negative) is an essential step in inner self-awareness.

Take some quiet moments to reflect on your capacities for constructive acting as well as your destructive potential toward yourself, your work, your family, and in your relationships.

Some of my constructive possibilities		*Some of my destructive possibilities*	
________	________	________	________
________	________	________	________
________	________	________	________

Positive and negative energies usually express themselves through your ego states. With self-contracts, you can find ways to channel your positive energies in ever-increasing amounts.

"I can't stand the freeway noise."

"This high humidity gets to me."

"I'm weak. I haven't eaten for six hours."

"Every time I'm around him I feel drained."

"I go over and over things in my head."

"I can't control myself."

Sometimes people's energies are drained off before they have a chance to use them. Most real problems in daily life can be traced to the habitual misuse of energy. People need to discover the blocks or "losses" in their inner core, that is, how energy is now being wasted.

Next to each common source of energy loss, indicate how serious an energy loss it is in your life. Note times, situations, people, and places where the loss tends to be greatest.

	Energy loss in me is			
Common sources of energy loss	*Bad and destructive*	*Worth being concerned about*	*Little or nothing*	*Times and places when energy loss is greatest*
Preoccupation with mistakes	( )	( )	( )	________
Depression	( )	( )	( )	________
Guilt	( )	( )	( )	________
Certain people	( )	( )	( )	________

	Energy loss in me is			
Common sources of energy loss	*Bad and destructive*	*Worth being concerned about*	*Little or nothing*	*Times and places when energy loss is greatest*
Anger	( )	( )	( )	________________
Dirty surroundings	( )	( )	( )	________________
Confusion	( )	( )	( )	________________
Fear	( )	( )	( )	________________
Loud noise	( )	( )	( )	________________
Self-punishment	( )	( )	( )	________________
Being put down	( )	( )	( )	________________
Anxiety, worry	( )	( )	( )	________________
Unfinished business	( )	( )	( )	________________
Expecting failure	( )	( )	( )	________________
Always wanting more	( )	( )	( )	________________
Feeling stupid	( )	( )	( )	________________
Overreacting	( )	( )	( )	________________
Being alone	( )	( )	( )	________________
Obsessions (I can't get my mind off it)	( )	( )	( )	________________
Crowds	( )	( )	( )	________________

Inner and outer energy losses

"I feel blocked on this job."

"I'm at the end of the road with no place to go."

"I'm shrivelled up inside."

"I'm tighter than a watch wound up too tight."

"When I say what I want, she just gets mad."

If people picture energies (biological, emotional, psychological, etc.) as flowing water, two forms of stopping the flow are apparent. Energy may be blocked from the outside or constricted from within. People, places, situations are common outer blocks. Anxiety, guilt, fear, lack of self-esteem, and the like are common inner constrictions. The Latin word for anxiety is *angustia,* which means "narrowness."

Reflect on the outer blocks and inner constrictions that most frequently create energy waste (loss) in you.

My outer blocks	*My inner constrictions*

Subsequent exercises will offer suggestions for dealing with blocks and constrictions.

"I'm always busy, that's my style."

"I prefer to take things easy."

"The doctor wants me to move to a one-story house."

"My husband wants me to do a lot of entertaining."

Daily life affects our flow of energy. Some people with boring jobs use energy just to keep going. Others' energies remain continually walled in and unused. Others continually expend energy doing emotionally exhausting things, such as working under stress conditions. Certain energy problems are inherent in certain life styles.

Review the energy patterns in your own life style. Note especially those situations that drain, block, or constrict your energy. Consider alternatives.

Situation	*Drains energy*	*Blocks energy*	*Constricts energy*	*Energy-conserving alternative*
________________	( )	( )	( )	________________
________________	( )	( )	( )	________________
________________	( )	( )	( )	________________
________________	( )	( )	( )	________________
________________	( )	( )	( )	________________
________________	( )	( )	( )	________________

Seldom discussed

"I don't want to talk about it."

"Why won't you sit down and discuss it with me?"

"Do you have to be so silent?"

"There isn't anything we can't tell each other."

Taboos, secrets, and "unmentionable" topics conceal or bottle up much of people's available energy. In addition, energy is consumed simply in keeping them hidden. "Getting behind" matters that are seldom discussed can release surprising amounts of personal inner-core energy.

Think of at least three topics at home, school, or at work that are seldom, if ever, discussed, but that you feel might be important to discuss. Then explain to yourself *why* the topic is not discussed or dealt with. What is at the root of the silence and avoidance?

Seldom-discussed topics	*How topics are avoided*	*Reason for avoidance*
________________	________________	________________
________________	________________	________________
________________	________________	________________
________________	________________	________________
________________	________________	________________
________________	________________	________________

"I feel so good back in the old home town."

"This kitchen feels friendly."

"I feel uncomfortable in high-rise buildings."

"Being in a crowded auditorium scares me."

Sometimes familiar surroundings trigger inner-core energy and vitality in people; sometimes familiar surroundings dampen energy and interest. It is helpful to know which situations are energizers and which are not.

Make two lists — one of the people, places, relationships, and situations that usually seem to allow energy to flow through you, and another of those that seem to dampen and block your energy.

Energizers	*De-energizers*
______________________	______________________
______________________	______________________
______________________	______________________
______________________	______________________
______________________	______________________

You may wish to make a self-contract to favor energizing situations and people in your life, and to avoid de-energizers as much as possible.

"When I'm with you I feel safe."

"You let me say anything I want. That's sure different."

"It's nice to be liked, even with a runny nose."

Being unconditionally *accepted for who you are* can help release energies from the inner core, because acceptance provides a context of freedom within which to live and operate. The very opposite seems generally true in the context of nonacceptance. When a person experiences nonacceptance, the inner core, with its basic urge to live, becomes constricted.

Make a note of all the people you can think of who accept you as you are. How do you feel when you are with them?

People who accept me	*How I feel when with them*	*People I accept*	*How I feel when with them*
___________	___________	___________	___________
___________	___________	___________	___________
___________	___________	___________	___________
___________	___________	___________	___________

Do you accept yourself here and now as a person who is valuable and important (at least to yourself)? ___________

If not, what do you need to do? ___________

"I hurt when people say, 'You've let me down.' "

"I hate it when my mother says, 'You'll never make it to the top.' "

"I turn on when people say they like me."

"I get excited when you say 'hello' in your special way."

Certain expressions people say *to* us or *about* us penetrate to the inner core. Supportive or encouraging things people say trigger positive energy in us, while negative expressions act as de-energizers. Recognizing such phrases helps people become aware of how their inner cores may be affected.

Make lists of expressions that are (1) positive energizers for you, and (2) negative energizers for you. If expressions are associated with particular persons, note their names.

Expressions that are positive energizers	*Person associated with it*
______________________	______________________
______________________	______________________

Expressions that are de-energizers	*Person associated with it*
______________________	______________________
______________________	______________________

You may need to self-contract to explore how concretely you are affected by what people say to you or about you.

"Let me know if I can be of help."

"I have an idea for you that might be useful."

"Let's go bicycling together!"

"Would you like to know what I think about solving that problem?"

You can begin accelerating energy flow between people by doing energizing things *for* them and *with* them. The delight in seeing energy used so productively will facilitate more personal and interpersonal energy.

Consider people in your life who can respond to your inner-core energies. Then, suggest ways you might encourage, support, and helpfully share with each of them.

People who respond to me	*Ways I can energize them*
____________________	____________________
____________________	____________________
____________________	____________________
____________________	____________________

Positive stroking has energy-releasing potential — both for others and for you.

"It's a new day. I wonder what I could try that's new."

"Maybe if I brainstorm the problem I'll come up with fresh answers."

"The children don't respond, so I need to experiment with a new approach."

Most people are energized by newness — a new relationship, new surroundings, a change in habits. New experiences open new perceptions and may open new avenues for the flow of inner-core energies.

Go back to the first chapter and review the various types of energy urges. Then consider: Where in your life could you explore a fresh approach? At home, at work, at school, in personal relationships, in television-watching habits, in reading habits? What energies might such a change release?

I could try a fresh approach in my	*Energies to be released*
______________________	______________________
______________________	______________________
______________________	______________________
______________________	______________________

You might want to make a self-contract to explore novelty as an energizer in your life.

"If I try that, what might happen?"

"It's time for something new, regardless."

"It's a risk. What do I have to gain?"

"What's in it for me?"

Investments of energy in people and personal projects usually bring profitable returns. Like investments in the stock market, such inner-core investments may be subject to losses as well as gains. The old adage, "Nothing ventured nothing gained," holds true here, but a wise self-contract can help keep losses to a minimum and gains to a maximum.

Think of two or three investments of your energy in the area of your life style that seem attractive to you and might bring profitable returns in inner-core energies. Also be aware of possible losses.

Investments of my energy	*Possible losses*	*Possible gains*

How might you self-contract such investments to minimize losses and maximize gains?

"I can moderate meetings well."

"Often I know when to shut up or speak up."

"When I concentrate, I work productively."

Inner energies are often channeled through a person's specific innate gifts and talents, as well as through skills and capacities they may have developed. Each person seems to have a different set of gifts. It is helpful for people to be in touch with their particular gifts and how they might be more fully used.

Make a list of your innate gifts and developed skills. Next to each, write how you presently exercise your gift or skill. Then, think of other ways each might be used to release even more inner energies.

My gifts and skills	*Ways I presently use them*	*Energizing ways I could use them*

You might like to design self-contracts to translate some of the third-column potentialities into actualities.

"I like basking in the sun."

"Walking in a soft fog reduces my tension."

"It's important to me to turn off my thinking occasionally and just be open to the universe."

"When I meditate, new meaning emerges for me."

Inner-core energies seem to respond favorably to moments of quiet and personal centeredness. Many people report that meditation and relaxation exercises help revitalize them.

Check those which apply.

	That's me	*That's not me*
I have a place where I can go to be quiet and centered.	( )	( )
I am familiar with some ways to relax my body and mind.	( )	( )
I can fit some moments (say 15 minutes per day) into my daily schedule for personal meditation and quiet.	( )	( )
I know that relaxing completely can help put me in touch with my energies.	( )	( )
I regularly use some form of relaxation and meditation.	( )	( )

Those statements which you marked "That's not me" might suggest areas for self-contracts, especially if you feel you could profit from revitalizing your energies.

Part Two

The Relating Self

11 Relationship Dynamics

The relating self

Humans are essentially interpersonal, instinctively motivated by an "urge to relate." They are meant to be beings-with-others, to find their meaning and purpose primarily *among* people. By interacting with others, they discover their own capacities and exercise their own skills. Their inner-core energies overflow into the lives of others.

In the dynamics of relating, communication plays a crucially important role.

> Once a human being has arrived on this earth, communication is the largest single factor determining what kinds of relationships he makes with others and what happens to him in the world about him.[1]

Through effective communication, people learn to express their feelings, to clarify problems, to resolve conflicts, to deal with value collisions. They learn to give compliments, present themselves attractively, give up playing psychological games, use their interpersonal time well, and achieve intimacy with important people in their lives.

For the most part, living is something humans do together, not alone. From the beginning, they have a *relating self* as well as an *individual self,* and they develop an interpersonal style as well as a personal one. They spend their lifetimes within a network of people, within which they learn to communicate with others. At the same time, they discover more about themselves by sharing experiences and working through conflicts with those around them.

Courage, motivation, and planning

Just as it takes courage, motivation, and planning to create a new *personal* self, these same three conditions are essential to creating a new *relating* self.

The *courage* required for interpersonal change is sometimes greater than that necessary for personal self-change. In personal change, the "enemy" is usually within — personal problems are usually familiar and predictable, and operate within well-known ego states. In contrast, interpersonal problems may be rooted in yourself, in others, or in your relationships with other people. Since the reactions of others are often unpredictable, the challenge to change is greater and may require more courage.

The *motivation* that influences personal self-change can enrich the motivation and meaning for interpersonal change as well. Changing your relating self usually, in turn, affects the lives of others. It may enliven friendships, enrich family ties, intensify work situations, help resolve conflicts, make people more attractive, overcome loneliness, build new relationships, create mutual interests, find shared meanings, uncover common values, and so on.

Planning for interpersonal change requires awareness of more ego states than your own. It requires thinking of *transactions* between two or more people rather than *personal actions and feelings* that don't necessarily involve other people. Interpersonal activities usually involve at least six ego states — your three and someone else's three.

Relationships plus

In the chapter "Personality Plus," the three ego states plus the inner core were presented as the essential parts of the self. Together they form the dynamic structure of the personal self.

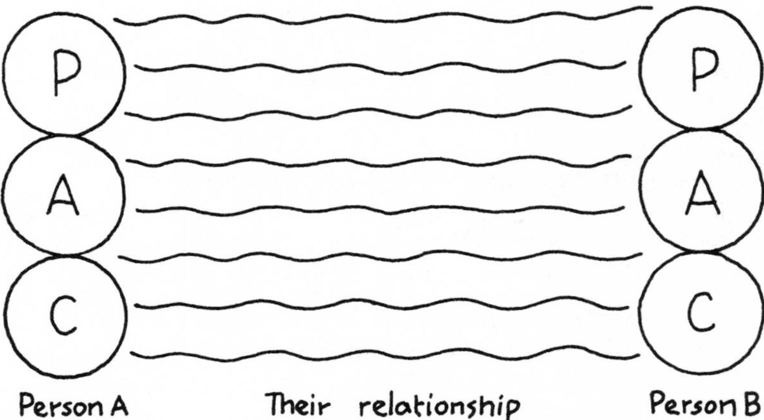

This chapter presents the dynamic structure of relationships, which involve an even more complex and elusive set of interactions. At the very least, three important elements need to be studied in an interpersonal relationship: the two (or more) relating persons plus *the relationship itself.*

The relationship itself can be explored, since it enjoys a reality of its own. While it does not exist if the relating people do not exist, it is not identical with either (or both) of them. The realm of "betweenness," as Martin Buber named it, is where a "relationship" comes into existence.

Like a marriage or close friendship, each relationship has a date of birth, which is independent of the birthdays of the two people relating. A relationship may continue to thrive while one of the relating partners founders through a difficult period of life. In short, a relationship possesses a life of its own.

On the other hand, a relationship does not have a flesh-and-bones existence. One cannot say, "here it is," or "there it is." Although it may grow and develop, it does not follow the rules of individual personality growth, nor are its needs (and there are plenty of them) experienced in quite the same way as personal needs. Everything takes place in a context of betweenness.

Like a personality, a relationship is always in process, shaped by the sharing, exchange, and blocking of personal energies. It is the product of changing personalities, and so its complexity is multiplied by the complexities of the relating persons.

Patterned, conflicting, and intimate relationships

Just as the personality has three styles of expressing itself — Parent, Adult, and Child — so relationships express themselves in three styles. These styles are characterized by *game patterns, conflicts,* and *intimacies.*

As noted earlier, an individual might be nurturing and caring from the Parent ego state, reasoning and informing from the Adult, and delighting and manipulative from the Child. Similarly, people-in-relationship might express their relationship in *patterned* interaction (such as games, rituals, stereotyped transactions, or other prescribed behaviors), in *conflict* interaction (such as in clashes over needs, interests, or values), and in *intimacy* interaction (as in open, creative, free, and loving situations).

Game patterns, conflicts, and intimacies can usually be recognized by analyzing transactions between ego states. However, because people can respond also with their inner cores, there is usually much more to understand in a relationship than mere interaction between ego states. The world of betweenness involves physical, psychological, and inner-core responses.

Just as the personality is permeated by an inner core, which energizes the three ego states, so a *relationship* may be permeated by the *inner-core energies* of the relating people. The positive exchange of inner-core energies can lead to what may be called core-to-core intimacy.

Some relating selves are thriving and happy; their relationships are rich with good experience. They find meaning and purpose in their friends, families, and associates. Inner-core energies are exchanged, flowing freely from one person to the other. Such people have healthy relating selves. Their relationships tend to be *open, intimate,* and *creative.*

Other people have relating selves that are week and unhealthy. Their relationships tend to be *closed, conflicting,* and filled with destructive *game playing.* The same meaningless experiences seem to happen to them over and over. Unresolved conflicts tend to grow and multiply like weeds. Inner-core energies are choked off or else are drained away in verbal collisions, feelings of rejection, fear of loneliness, and so on, until hardly any energy remains for building strong, supportive relationships.

A healthy relating self

This second part of *A New Self* is designed to help people develop a healthy relating self and feel at home in the dimension of betweenness.

First, it shows you how to get in touch with certain relationships characterized by conflicts and games. It also shows how to identify the ways people close themselves off from intimacy or block potentially good relationships.

Second, Part II suggests ways to *de-game* relationships in which partners play destructive psychological games; to *resolve conflicts* in relationships where partners habitually cross each other; and to *open* relationships to healthier ways of interacting, once games and conflict patterns have been uncovered.

Third, it demonstrates how, in the world of betweenness, a person may enjoy many different relationships, yet since each relationship has a life of its own, its needs may need to be structured or, in many cases, restructured. Suggestions for developing core-to-core intimacy are offered in those relationships where such closeness is possible and desirable.

Throughout this part of the book, the self-contract format will continue to be useful. In addition, an *interpersonal contract* format, presented later in this chapter, offers a formula for interpersonal change to be used when two or more people agree to change in their relationship.

A creative process

Developing a new relating self is a creative activity, because in a number of ways it involves bringing something *new* into being.

In one way, this creative process involves new expressions of *interpersonal values,* like intimacy, friendship, and responsibility for others. Such shared values come alive when people relate creatively.

This creative process also releases new *interpersonal energies* in the relating persons, such as trusting, caring, sharing, loving, thinking together, and the like. This process of developing a new relating self helps people *communicate more effectively.* And perhaps most important, the process also opens the way for people who relate intimately and openly to develop an "extra self" — *a third self* — a shared self that exists in the dimension of betweenness. This "third self," the focus of a later chapter, possesses its unique "personality" and may be diagrammed as:

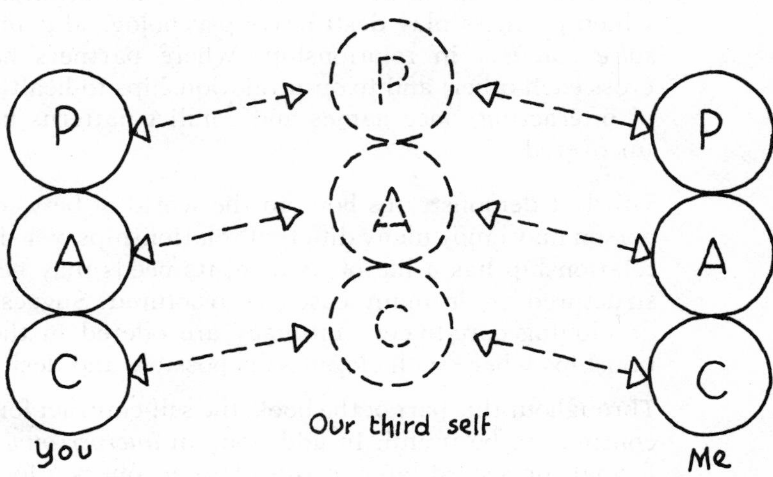

Bringing into being new values and energies, new and more effective lines of communication, and new "third selves" are among the most exciting challenges of interpersonal change and creative relationships.

"I wish I could share my feelings with him more easily."

"I want to recognize her nonverbal messages more clearly."

"What a team we would make if we could really *think together!*"

Many people feel that some of their relationships would be creative if only they could improve their communication in one or two areas. They look forward to exciting, stimulating relationships at home, at work, among friends. And sometimes such creative relationships are quite within their reach, once they clarify key problem areas and make some shared agreements to change.

This exercise helps you get in touch with some of your potentially creative relationships.

Are there people in your life with whom you would like to enjoy freer and deeper relationships? If so, who are they? What are some areas in each relationship where you would like to see improvement happen, knowing that it would make the relationship more stimulating and creative?

Names	*Desired areas of communication improvement*
____________________	______________________________________
____________________	______________________________________
____________________	______________________________________

"I can't stand fat people."

"I am fascinated by men with dark eyes."

"He's always rubbing his nose the way my father used to do. Ugh."

"I hate people who always talk about themselves."

A person's likes or dislikes generally have a long history. Certain preferences may even have childhood origins. Whatever their source, it helps to be conscious of your own personal preferences.

People can often clarify some of their own personal relating problems by first observing how other people show preferences. For example, first impressions are significant. Certain people seem to attract, others to repel. But not everybody would agree on what attracts and what repels. It seems to be a matter of individual taste.

What kinds of people do you feel comfortable with? What is it about their words, behavior, or appearance that attracts you to them?

Kinds of people	*What specifically attracts me*
______________________	______________________
______________________	______________________

What kinds of people do you least like to interact with? What is it about them you seem to dislike?

Kinds of people	*What specifically I dislike*
______________________	______________________
______________________	______________________

"I have been *trying* to understand you for years."
"You certainly don't show it."

"You never seem to grasp what I'm trying to say."
"You're too emotional when you talk."

Interpersonal problems are frequently communication problems. The people involved may want to work together, live together, or love each other effectively, but something happens along the way to prevent the desired outcome.

Sometimes misunderstandings are merely miscommunications that can be clarified.

Do you sometimes find it difficult to let others know what you really mean? Specify some people with whom you've experienced misunderstanding and/or miscommunication.

Names	*Situations where difficulties happen*
____________________	______________________________________
____________________	______________________________________

Can you think of people you relate to who seem to find it difficult getting you to understand them? People whom you misunderstand?

Names	*Situations where difficulties happen*
____________________	______________________________________
____________________	______________________________________
____________________	______________________________________
____________________	______________________________________

"I can't deal with her when she throws a tantrum."

"My friend is *always* trying to help me and won't let me do anything for myself."

Once people are willing to admit interpersonal problems exist, they are on the way to resolving them.

Next, different problems need to be identified *as different*. Interacting with a chronic complainer is quite different from interacting with an incurable optimist. Both situations can create problems in relating, but each calls for a different approach, a unique solution. Therefore, the problem area needs to be pinpointed.

Check those interpersonal problem areas that concern you at this time. How do you typically respond?

Typical problem areas dealing with . . .	*Specific people with whom I have this problem*	*My typical response*
( ) angry people	______	______
( ) pessimistic people	______	______
( ) overly emotional people	______	______
( ) people who cheat and lie	______	______
( ) unemotional people	______	______
( ) Victim role players	______	______
( ) Persecutor role players	______	______
( ) Rescuer role players	______	______

"I'm willing to work at it, are you?"

"We're taking a communication course together."

"I don't know how you feel. Will you tell me?"

When problems occur in a relationship, it is important to clarify whether an *individual* has the problem, or whether it is a shared problem that belongs to the *relationship.*

When one person owns the problem, that person may need to self-contract in order to resolve the problem.

When both people in the relationship share a problem, they will need to cooperate in seeking a solution. It is important that they reach the point where both *agree* that they share a problem in relationship, and both are *willing to work together* to solve it.

Among the people with whom you would like to develop a more open and effective relationship at home, at work, etc., are there any who *share with you* a desire to improve the relationship?

Those who would work with me to improve our relationship	*What we each need to do*
______________________	______________________
______________________	______________________
______________________	______________________

Using personal and interpersonal contracts

The self-contract can often be used in interpersonal situations, when persons can improve a relationship simply by changing their own attitudes and behavior, *as individuals,* without requiring the involvement of relating partners.

The self-contract may also be used when partners refuse to cooperate in making mutual changes, or when one person is physically, psychologically, or emotionally incapable of cooperating, such as during periods of illness or severe emotional distress. At times like these, the willing and capable individual may still initiate a self-change, and in this way improve the interpersonal situation.

However, when people agree to cooperate in change and decide to work together at improving their relationship, an *interpersonal contract* is more appropriate. The interpersonal contract takes into account the different needs, values, desires, capacities, and histories of the contracting persons.

The interpersonal contract form is much like a traditional business agreement, since it involves two or more people with separate interests, who have different goods, services, and skills to contract about. At each step in the interpersonal contract, viewpoints of at least two people are taken into account. And, while both parties to the agreement may agree about the *area* of their relationship they wish to improve, they may disagree about the *way* to do it. For example, two friends may agree that they would like to spend more time together. But one friend wants the "more time" to happen exclusively during the day, while the other desires it to happen during the evening.

Finding areas of compatibility will usually be the first challenge people face when designing an interpersonal contract.

The next challenge will be for the contracting parties to formulate their agreements in ways that are *reasonable, measurable,* and *practical.* This is often a difficult step, both in self-contracts and in interpersonal ones. It may require practice.

1. In what *general area* of our present relationship would we like to make a change? ______________________
2. How would each of us describe the successful outcome of the contract? What is each of us looking for specifically? (It may be different for each person to the contract.)

   1st person ______________________

   2nd person* ______________________
3. Do our goals or outcomes fit together in some way? Are they compatible? ______________________

   a) If yes, specify how they fit ______________________

   ____

   b) If the goals fit together *only partially,* then design a modified agreement.

   c) If the goals don't fit, don't take the next step until you've reworked the first three points so that your goals are compatible. If this is impossible, you may be able to make *separate self-contracts.*
4. Following is our agreement, stated reasonably, measurably, and practically.

   Agreement of 1st person ______________________

   ____

   Agreement of 2nd person ______________________

   ____
5. What are each of us willing to do to effect the change?

   1st person ____________ 2nd person ____________

   ____________ ____________

   ____________ ____________

*More lines may be added at each step when more than two persons are contracting.

6. What personal skills, talents, abilities, or native gifts do each of us have that would facilitate our planned change?

   1st person ____________ 2nd person ____________

   ____________ ____________

   ____________ ____________

7. How might the progress of our contract be measured separately, and charted together?

   1st person ____________

   2nd person ____________

   Together ____________

8. How will others come to know about the change we're making in our relationship? ____________

9. How will we know when our contract has been fulfilled?

   ____

10. How might we sabotage our contract separately or together?

    1st person ____________

    2nd person ____________

    Together ____________

11. Would others, knowing about our contract, tend to help or hinder its fulfillment or effectiveness?

    Who might help *Who might hinder*

    ____________ ____________

    ____________ ____________

    ____________ ____________

12. What might be done about anyone who might hinder our contract?

    ____

13. Will our parental values, principles, traditions, and rules of life tend to support or sabotage the contract?

1st Person		*2nd Person*	
Supportive Parent	*Sabotaging Parent*	*Supportive Parent*	*Sabotaging Parent*
________	________	________	________
________	________	________	________
________	________	________	________

14. Will our childhood training, experiences, and feelings tend to support or sabotage the contract?

1st Person		*2nd Person*	
Supportive Child	*Sabotaging Child*	*Supportive Child*	*Sabotaging Child*
________	________	________	________
________	________	________	________
________	________	________	________

15. Is our contract revisable if revision seems

    necessary? ______________________________

    If so, how? ______________________________

    ____

Helpful hints

Some people enter into contracts when they feel dissatisfaction in some area of their lives, others only when they experience a crisis. In each case, if they do so willingly, they are likely to fulfill their contracts.

When people are forced into an interpersonal contract (like a shotgun marriage), its successful fulfillment might be more easily sabotaged.

In general, although a contract sabotage may come from external sources, it frequently comes from the Parent or Child ego state.

When the Child is very displeased with a contract statement, some "goodies" may need to be included in the revision to please the Child — for example, a pleasure reward for the Natural Child, a curiosity reward for the Little Professor, and an approval reward for the Adapted Child.

If a contract meets with mild Parent disapproval, it may not need to be revised, but merely restated in a more traditional way.

Sometimes it is impossible to revise a contract in any way that would receive the approval of the inner Parent, especially if the person's real parents were emotionally disturbed or disliked the individual during childhood. In such cases, the Adult needs to:

- act as a strong referee, stronger than the Parent, so that the destructive Parent cannot get to the Child and reward the Child for performance,
- placate the disapproving Parent by "throwing a crumb" to it, that is, by planning to do some little thing that would please the Parent and somehow make it less resistant, or
- take time to do self re-Parenting so that the contract would meet the approval of the New Parent.

No guarantee

Fulfilling a contract does not guarantee that a relationship will improve, any more than taking a particular medicine is a guaranteed cure for a particular illness. People frequently misidentify an interpersonal contract (for example, to take a communication course) with their desired goal (to become closer friends).

People cannot *contract* to become closer friends, any more than businessmen can write a contract to become millionaires. In both cases, the desired goal (to become closer friends, to become millionaires) is a source of motivation, urging people to construct *effective contracts* that will eventually help bring about the desired goal.

12 Strokes and Stroking

The effect of strokes

Infants need to be held, touched, stroked, cuddled, loved, fondled, fed, and cared for almost continuously. Touching and recognition make a baby feel loved and wanted. In a positive atmosphere, children can develop a positive sense of self-awareness and self-esteem. Research has shown that long before infants have words with which to express themselves, they are able to identify familiar faces and respond to smiles. They like to be recognized and to be liked.

In the process of growing up, people learn to accept substitute strokes for those received in infancy. A handshake, for example, may replace the warm hug. Yet grownups, like infants, need to be recognized positively and valued for being who they are as well as for what they do. They need "strokes."

Many people structure their time so as to be with people they like whenever possible. They do this to get strokes. They tend to feel safer and more open with people whom they value and who value them, instead of people who are indifferent or hostile.

Strokes and OKness

In an atmosphere of OKness and affirmation, people can laugh together (in their Child ego states), can gather information and solve problems together (in their Adult ego states), and can express traditions and share opinions (in their Parent ego states). In an accepting climate, they are motivated to help each other on a project, care for each other in time of trouble, and ask for assistance and get it.

Some people are enjoyable to be with. The feelings they express are affirming of others, the messages they communicate, with both words and gestures, are welcoming and open. The vibrations that emanate from them are comforting and alive. Such people encourage others to feel good. According to TA, the art of encouraging others to feel affirmed, alive, alert, and important is called "positive stroking."

Other people are simply not enjoyable to be with. The feelings they express are unsettling and the messages they transmit are unwelcoming. Their "vibes" make others feel uncomfortable. Such people are often cool and repellent, or hostile and combative. According to TA, they practice the art of "negative stroking."

In this chapter on stroking, you will begin to discover why you like to spend time with the warm and friendly people in your life, and why you find yourself avoiding interpersonal relationships that make you feel not-OK and insignificant. You will get in touch with your own need to be touched, liked, valued, and welcomed as a person who relates, and you will learn how to recognize these same kinds of needs in others. You will discover ways to enrich your relating self through stroking. The art of positive stroking is undoubtedly one of the best skills you can learn to enhance the interpersonal dimension in your life. Positive strokers tend to create happy, healthy relationships.

Positive stroking is one of the most universally useful processes for acquiring a new self. It helps people, personally and interpersonally, to become more and more OK. For those who already feel OK, stroking strengthens their self-image and motivates them to develop their potentials more fully.

In the process of everyday life, people continually give and receive strokes, both positive and negative ones. Those who habitually and unthinkingly give negative strokes may end up destroying their interpersonal lives. Positive strokers tend to have attractive personalities. Their positive *target strokes* nurture OKness in those they stroke, and in themselves as well.

Positive and negative strokes

"When you talk to me like that, I melt."

"You never say anything nice to me."

"Touch me, just touch me."

"Hi there, you all."

A stroke is defined as an act of recognition. Greetings and handshakes are common strokes. Strokes may be given verbally or nonverbally. Some nonverbal strokes, such as smiles, are positive; others, such as frowns, are negative. Being greeted by name is a positive verbal stroke. Having one's name mispronounced is a negative verbal stroke.

Everybody needs strokes to survive. Everybody gets them and gives them. Positive strokes are like "warm fuzzies" and feel good. Negative strokes are like "cold pricklies" that hurt and irritate.[1] Some strokes, positive or negative, are more effective than others.

Think of the last two days and the people with whom you interacted. Observe the stroking patterns.

Warm fuzzies I received	*Cold pricklies I received*	*Warm fuzzies I gave others*	*Cold pricklies I gave others*
____________	____________	____________	____________
____________	____________	____________	____________
____________	____________	____________	____________
____________	____________	____________	____________

Conditional and unconditional strokes

"I'm glad you're you."

"If you'd get better grades, I'd like you better."

"You'll have to change if you want me to stay around."

"I'd love to go out to dinner with you — after you help me fix my hair dryer."

Strokes may be given conditionally or unconditionally. A *conditional* stroke includes a *demand* for some kind of behavior. The demand, stated or implied, sends the message, "I approve of you if you. . . ."

Common demands include: work harder, act sexier, make more money, get better grades, etc.

An *unconditional* stroke includes no demands. It's message, stated or implied, is, "I love you because you're you," or "I accept you as a person." Seemingly, it is easier to get conditional strokes than unconditional ones. However, both kinds can be meaningful and valuable in relationships.

Compare the kinds of strokes you received in childhood with the ones you get currently. Also compare the ones you gave then and give now.

Receiving Strokes

Conditional strokes I received in childhood	*Conditional strokes I receive currently*
_________________________	_________________________
_________________________	_________________________
_________________________	_________________________

Unconditional strokes I received in childhood

Unconditional strokes I receive currently

Giving Strokes

Conditional strokes I gave in childhood

Conditional strokes I give currently

Unconditional strokes I gave in childhood

Unconditional strokes I give currently

The necessity for strokes

"Mama, why do people get little when they get old?"

"I feel cold, like withdrawing from life."

"At least I get attention when we fight."

"I always knew I was loved."

A common TA saying is: "Without strokes a person's spinal cord shrivels up."[2] In other words, strokes are absolutely necessary for survival. Sometimes young children who do not get enough positive strokes will "act up" in ways to provoke negative strokes. Having others notice them is so vital for their existence that they are willing to settle for cold pricklies when they can't get warm fuzzies, since being deprived of recognition is the worst state of all. Children who are ignored and radically stroke-deprived often do not develop in healthy ways — physically or emotionally.

Later in life, people who have received an abundance of positive strokes are likely to have positive scripts. Those who receive many negative strokes or are deprived of strokes will usually have negative scripts. People go through life looking for strokes, although they're often unaware that they do so.

Become aware of what you do to collect strokes. Think of the last twenty-four hours. See yourself as though on TV. Observe your patterns of giving and getting strokes. If you like what you see, keep on doing what you're doing. If there's room for improvement, consider the contracts you need to make.

"Wow, what you said really makes me happy."

"That's the worst thing you could say to me right now."

"What can I give you that you really want?"

Some strokes people give seem to hit the target.[3] Positive target strokes are exactly what a person longs for; negative target strokes are exactly what a person fears and wants to avoid. "Being abandoned" is a commonly feared negative target stroke. Being listened to with empathy and understanding is a commonly sought-after positive target stroke.

Begin to get in touch with the target strokes that hurt you or enhance you.

Words or phrases that hurt me the most are ______________

____

Things people do that really hurt me are ______________

____

Words or phrases that make me feel really good are ______

____

Things people do that really make me feel good are ______

____

The target stroke I most fear is ______________

The target stroke I most want is ______________

"But you promised me."

"Don't leave me, mama, please stay."

"I feel so good cuddled up beside you."

"Chocolate ice cream was just what I wanted."

The most common target strokes that people are aware of are those they receive in the Child ego state.

Strokes that involve touching or eating usually target the Natural Child. The Little Professor may be target stroked for its creativity and use of intuition, while strokes of approval or disapproval usually hit the target of the Adapted Child. Sarcasm and broken promises are but two of the negative target strokes to the Adapted Child. Trustworthiness and compliments are two positive target strokes to the Adapted Child.

Go back in memory to your childhood. Analyze how each part of your Child was stroked when you were little.

	Strokes	*Liked or disliked*	*Would have preferred*
Natural Child	______	______	______
	______	______	______
Little Professor	______	______	______
	______	______	______
Adapted Child	______	______	______
	______	______	______

Star those strokes that hit the target in you, either positively or negatively.

"If you get good grades, I'll be very pleased."

"The way you can please me best is to be quiet."

"I've always wanted you to be a priest."

Parent figures that people have when they are young become their Parent ego states as they grow older. People who listen to their inner dialogues can often hear their parents' hopes, fears, or demands. When people comply with or rebel against these Parent messages, they often give their Parents a target stroke. Doing things that would please their parents, such as carrying on family traditions, are positive target strokes to the Parent. Doing things that would hurt or anger their parents, like rejecting family traditions, are negative target strokes.

Recall childhood strokes that would hit the target in your parents. When you were little, what about you most

pleased your parents? ______________________________

What most displeased them? ______________________________

Are there people in your current life who you expect to please or displease you (your Parent ego state) as you once did

your parents? ______________________________

What do you think about that? ______________________________

____

____

____

"That's a well-thought-out program."

"Working with you is a positive experience."

"I like the way you dress for the job."

Historically, women have received many strokes for having a nurturing Parent ego state and having an obedient or sexy Child, while men have been abundantly stroked for Adult achievement. Currently, this pattern is changing. Many people today are looking for different kinds of strokes. For example, more and more women want recognition for their thinking Adult abilities, while more and more men want recognition for their nurturing Parent abilities and acceptance for their Child.

Watch TV, think of movies you've recently seen, or look through some magazines, noting how people act or how they are depicted. Record the strokes given to a person in the Adult ego state for rational thinking and behavior.

Strokes to the Adult in women	*Strokes to the Adult in men*
______________________	______________________
______________________	______________________
______________________	______________________
______________________	______________________

"I'm so scared to ask my husband for what I want."

"I'll do it even if I'm shaking."

"Once I get started, it's not so hard."

It often takes courage to change stroking patterns. Many people are afraid that they won't get what they ask for, so they don't ask. Or, they are afraid that if they give people more strokes, their strokes will be rejected.

These people do not feel courageous and often do not act it. Courage may be described as *acting positively in spite of internal fear.*

Fear is often unrealistic, a feeling coming from the past and unrelated to the present. Fill in the following blanks.

I want to get a ______________ stroke from ______________.
(describe) (name)

I don't ask for it because I'm afraid of ______________.

The worst thing that could happen if my stroking fears are actualized is ______________________________

What I need to do to get the strokes I want is to __________

instead of __________ which I am now doing.

"Why should I? It wouldn't make any difference."

"If I smile, the world might smile back."

"Everything would have more meaning if someone would love me."

People are motivated to change when they receive healthy strokes. Stroking may also help clarify and enrich the meaning and value of a relationship. Getting strokes from parents or peers often motivates children into action and, similarly, when children stroke their parents, the parents may be motivated into action. Most people welcome approval and respond by seeking further successes and additional positive strokes.

Sometimes people have high motivation, sometimes low, sometimes so-so. They may say they want something very much, yet are unwilling to work to achieve their goal. Consequently, their chances for success are minimal.

Strokes I want	*Chances of getting strokes I want*	*What I'm willing to do to get what I want*	*My level of motivation*
___	___	___	___
___	___	___	___
___	___	___	___
___	___	___	___

A contract plan for strokes

"I'm going to do it tomorrow."

"If I start small, I'll have a better chance of success."

"I'm going all out on my new plan."

If you've read this far in this book and have worked through most of the exercises, you are probably becoming more and more aware of how you can set contracts, achieve them, or sabotage them. You have probably been making self-contracts and have studied the interpersonal contract form.

Interpersonal contracts seem to be more effective when the contracting parties give and receive some positive stroking.

Write out a plan for getting and giving more positive strokes. For example, you might plan each day to compliment your co-workers or say "hello" and smile at five people you might normally avoid or not notice. If their eyes light up, you will have hit the target.

Strokes I plan to give	*To whom*	*How I'll evaluate*
____________	____________	____________
____________	____________	____________

Strokes I plan to get	*From whom*	*How I'll evaluate*
____________	____________	____________
____________	____________	____________

"I like the way I handled that personnel problem."

"Hey, I look pretty good in this bathing suit."

"I'm a darn good cook — my apple pie can't be beat."

It's great to receive target strokes from other people. Unfortunately, other people aren't always around to give you the strokes you need. At times like these, positive self-stroking helps develop a stronger new self. Self-stroking is a skill to be learned. Many people, recognizing their own negative qualities, often give themselves negative strokes. It would be more helpful if they could discover ways to self-stroke from a positive position. When people self-stroke positively, they are recognizing their potential strengths and *focusing* on their strengths rather than on their weaknesses.

Consider your activities during the last 24 hours. Recall how you talked to yourself and gave yourself strokes.

Negative strokes I gave myself	*Positive strokes I gave myself*
______________________	______________________
______________________	______________________

Strokes I need to get from me	*What I would have to do to get them*
______________________	______________________
______________________	______________________

Star the strokes that had, or would have, the most meaning for you.

Notes

Chervet

Games and De-Gaming

Why people play games

Everyone plays psychological games at times. Like solitaire, games can be played singly; like chess, they can be two-handed; like basketball, a number of players may be involved.

In every case, the players have some "under the surface" awareness of the rules and choose to play, *often because they don't know any better*. Most people are trained not to ask directly for what they want or need from others. So, some hint at their needs by looking sad and acting helpless, or by stamping their feet and acting angry, or by smiling hopefully and acting encouragingly. Others get what they want by verbally manipulating those around them.

People usually manipulate others not because they want to, but because they don't know what to do instead. Or, they are afraid their direct requests will be ignored, ridiculed, or punished in some way.

People play psychological games because they learn to do so in childhood. It feels safer to be evasive and indirect about one's needs than to risk the rejection that could follow a straightforward request.

The common dramatic roles — Victim, Persecutor, and Rescuer — are played out as minidramas in each game, with players usually switching roles as the game progresses.

At the end of a game, one or more of the players involved collects negative feelings, such as anger, depression, confusion, or hurt. Sometimes a game player collects a self-righteous feeling, feels blameless, and accuses others of playing games.

Games can be broken up when people stop exaggerating their own, or other people's, strengths and weaknesses, and work directly for the positive pay-offs that follow negative games. Being direct and open often takes courage, yet directness gives new meaning to relationships.

How games are learned

According to Eric Berne, games are patterns learned in early childhood and are passed on from one generation to the next.

"The favored game of any individual can be traced back to his parents and grandparents, and forward to his children; they in turn, unless there is a successful intervention, will teach them to their grandchildren."[1]

Games are learned by imitation and assignment. When *imitating* games of their parents, children play identical roles and repeat the same lines. When games are *assigned,* usually without the parents' awareness, children learn to play the expected role. For example, a young child who is severely punished for spilling milk and *not* forgiven may decide to try to be perfect and never make mistakes, and is likely to play the game, *Look How Hard I'm Trying.* Another child who is severely punished for spilling milk and who *is* forgiven may continue the same pattern throughout life, making messes, apologizing, and expecting to be forgiven. This becomes the game of *Schlemiel.* Although *Schlemiel* is usually a two-person game, it can be played as a solitary game. In such cases, the Adapted Child will make a mess, then apologize inwardly if an old Parent tape is critical of the mess, then feel good if a nurturing Parent tape says something like, "Don't worry, everyone makes mistakes sometimes." Thus, the game that is played inwardly is reinforced so that it can be played once more in an interpersonal situation.

Game patterns

Games in TA theory may be described as:

- a series of complementary transactions at the social level
- a series of ulterior transactions at the psychological level
- a pay-off of negative feelings for one or both players at the end of the series of transactions.

Transactions between people, in which more than one message is being communicated, are commonly diagrammed in the following way: *solid lines* indicate the social (or obvious verbal) interaction usually expressed in the *words* people use; *broken lines* indicate the psychological (ulterior) transaction, usually expressed in the *feelings* people communicate.

A common game, *Why don't you, Yes but* has an easily recognized pattern. It can be diagrammed as:

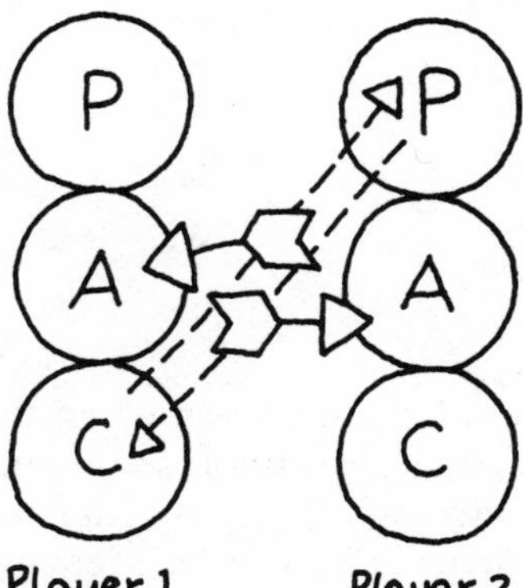

Player 1: (looking sad) I have a problem...

Player 2: (looking concerned) Why don't you...

Player 1: (still sad) Yes, but that won't work because...

Player 2: (still concerned) Then why don't you...

The game continues. Player 1 rejects all helpful suggestions until Player 2 feels inadequate and becomes frustrated, according to the pattern of suggestion-followed-by-its-rejection, at not being able to help. Thus, the game ends. Not every request for help or offer of help is a game. When people accept suggestions and carry them out successfully, it is not a game.

Games in the drama of life

One of the important reasons for learning about games is because they are such an important part of any script. Game patterns, like short scenes in a lengthy drama, reveal the characters and theme, and move the play toward its inevitable end. If games are de-escalated or given up in favor of openness, the script takes on new meaning.

This chapter offers techniques for understanding games, for identifying game patterns, and for de-gaming. De-gaming is learning how to live without games in a society which pressures people to keep on playing games and, at times, can scarcely tolerate the authenticity of a new self.

"She's always picking on me."

"Yes, but all the other kids get to go."

"I was only trying to help you."

"He started it first."

Children learn to play psychological games when they are very young. Long before they enter school, some children learn games that involve blaming others in order to avoid being responsible for their own actions. Others learn games in which they take *all* the blame when things go wrong. They assume they're always at fault and, as a result, take on too much responsibility. Children who frequently blame others often feel self-righteous or justified in feeling angry. Children who frequently accept blame often feel depressed, inadequate, or guilty. They believe they can never do enough to please others.

List responsibilities you were supposed to assume as a child — those you accepted, those you rejected. Include things such as cleaning your room, caring for a pet or a person, personal hygiene, etc.

My childhood responsibilities	*The responsibilities seemed: reasonable or unreasonable*	*What I did with the responsibilities and my feelings*

"You're always putting me down. What do I do wrong?"

"Why don't you ever get things right!"

Games have themes and names. Common ones are:

Theme of the game	*Name of the game*
Being "too busy" to complete things well.	Harried
Frequently getting disapproval from people.	Kick Me
Not able to please someone, no matter what.	Cornered
Continually being available to help others.	I'm Only Trying to Help You
Nit-picking and frequently finding little things wrong.	Blemish
Waiting for people to make mistakes, then pouncing.	Now I've Got You, You S.O.B.
Exploiting a misfortune to avoid responsibility.	Wooden Leg
Taking out more and more loans and credit cards.	Debtor

Think of some things that happen to you over and over again (the theme). Make up a name that summarizes the action.

The game theme	*Name of the game*
____________________	____________________
____________________	____________________
____________________	____________________

"It's all your fault that dinner burned."

"No matter what I do, I'm always wrong."

"You can always count on me to be helpful."

The drama roles of Victim, Persecutor, and Rescuer are present in all games and a switch in roles is always part of the game. The following dialogue illustrates the process.[2]

Son: (as Persecutor, yells angrily at mother)	You know I hate blue. Here you went and bought me another blue shirt!
Mother: (as Victim)	I never do anything right as far as you're concerned.
Father: (rescues mother, persecutes son)	Don't you dare yell at your mother like that, young man. Go to your room and no dinner!
Son: (now as Victim sulking in his room)	They tell me to be honest, and when I tell them what I don't like, they put me down. How can you satisfy people like that?
Mother: (now Rescuer, sneaks him a tray of food)	Now don't tell your father. We shouldn't get so upset over a shirt.
Mother: (returning to father as Persecutor)	John, you're so tough with our son. I'll bet he's sitting in his room right now hating you.
Father: (as Victim)	Gee, honey, I was only trying to help you, and you kick me where it hurts the most.
Son: (calling out as Rescuer)	Hey, Mom, lay off, will ya? Dad's just tired.

To get in touch with situations where you usually play the drama roles of Rescuer, Persecutor, and Victim, complete the following:

People I feel like helping	*What I do or say*	*Their response to me*	*A game or not a game?*
______	______	______	______
______	______	______	______

People I feel critical of	*What I do or say*	*Their response to me*	*A game or not a game?*
______	______	______	______
______	______	______	______

People I feel victimized by	*What I do or say*	*Their response to me*	*A game or not a game?*
______	______	______	______
______	______	______	______

"You're trying to con me."

"She really pulled a switch on me."

"I responded, then look what I got."

The game formula, which was first clarified by Eric Berne,[3] shows that games start when one player tries to "con" another. If the second player can be conned and responds as expected, the game is on. During the game, the first player pulls an unexpected switch, often a change in roles. It disconcerts the second player, who then collects a negative feeling. This feeling is the pay-off that ends the game.

The game formula is:

$$C + G = R \rightarrow S \rightarrow X \rightarrow P$$

C = the con, the ulterior message player 1 sends to player 2.

G = the gimmick, a weak spot in player 2, such as self-righteousness, sentimentality, criticalness, or cruelty.

R = the response player 2 makes if hooked.

S = the switch, which is an unexpected move by player 1.

X = the cross-up, which is player 2 being thrown off balance because of the unexpected switch.

P = the pay-off that each player receives (negative feelings about self or self-righteous feelings in relation to other people).

Common "cons" people use on you	*Your common responses to the cons*	*How the situation ends up*
__________	__________	__________
__________	__________	__________
__________	__________	__________

Rapo: a sexual and social game

"Why don't you come up and see me sometime?"

"Wow, you sure look sexy tonight."

"Keep your hands to yourself."

"And I thought I could trust you."

Rapo is a common game in which the initiating player enjoys making the other person feel like a fool. In the game of sexual Rapo, one person hints (Child to Child) that he or she is sexually available. If the other person responds as expected, the Rapo player often switches from Sexy Child to Critical Parent and rejects the second player. The Rapo player then feels triumphant and self-righteous, saying aloud or inwardly, "People like that are always after sex." The second player caught up in the game feels depressed, inadequate, or angry and often cannot understand what went wrong when everything looked so promising at first.

The game of Rapo can also be played socially, in a nonsexual way. The dynamics are the same. One person seemingly offers something, then withdraws the offer when someone else expresses a wish for it.

Describe a situation in which someone seemingly promised you something or delivered a nonverbal come-on, and then pulled a switch when you responded. How did you feel about it and what did you do with your feelings?

____

____

____

"That nosy neighbor of yours has been saying you're not fit to be a mother."

"You're not going to let him get away with that, are you!"

"Say, if you knew what she said about you, you'd be furious."

The game of *Let's You and Him Fight* is a three-handed game. It is initiated by a troublemaker, often a gossip who wants other people to fight. If successful in generating an argument, the initiator of the game sits back and takes vicarious pleasure in observing the fight. He or she often feels superior to the two combatants, knowing what a phony setup it has been.

If, for example, the initiator is a woman who wants two men to fight over her, she may choose a third admirer instead to make the other two feel foolish. That's the pay-off, making others feel foolish. Naturally, the game is also initiated by men who want women to fight over them or by anyone who wants to start a fight between two or more people, only to then ridicule them while staying emotionally detached oneself.

Recall a time when a troublemaker invited you into an argument with three or more persons.

What did the troublemaker do? ______________________________

Then what happened? ______________________________

How did it end up for each person involved? ______________________________

____

"I often feel confused and don't understand."

"I always end up feeling hurt."

"Guilty is the way I usually feel."

At the end of any game, one or both persons end up with a negative feeling. This feeling may be depression, confusion, hurt, guilt, or anger, or perhaps a feeling of blamelessness or self-righteousness.

Some people are not in touch with their feelings — they are skilled at blocking or denying them day after day. In spite of this, their bodies may be saving up the feelings. Like money in the bank collecting interest, a person may eventually save up enough anger, for example, to develop ulcers. The longer a person holds on to negative feelings, instead of working them through, the larger is the "prize" he or she feels justified in collecting.

Compare your collections of feelings in childhood with those you collect now.

Feelings I often had when things went wrong in childhood

were ____

Feelings I often have when things go wrong *currently* are __

____

I still remember feeling very ______________________

about ____

that happened when I was ________ years old. I sometimes

feel the same when ______________________ happens.

The game plan

"Whenever my mother-in-law drops by to chat, one of us ends up feeling hurt."

"Every time I ask to borrow the car, we get in the same argument."

"I can't seem to break out of the pattern."

The Game Plan[4] is a way to identify repetitive games that often permeate a script. It is presented as a series of five questions:

1. What keeps happening over and over in your life that leaves someone feeling badly?
2. How does the pattern start?
3. What happens next?
4. How does it end?
5. How does each person feel when it ends?

The Game Plan also helps pinpoint ways to break up the games, thus changing the balance of the script. It is based on the principle that each game has a plan, much like the plans football players formulate for each of their plays. A plan follows a predictable pattern, with a pay-off at the end. Following is an example of the Game Plan.

Sis:	(Asks a favor.)
Pa:	No.
Sis:	Why not?
Pa:	Because, last time you . . . (put down) . . .
Sis:	Well, that's not true . . .
Pa and Sis:	(Argue loudly.)
Sis:	(Leaves the room, yelling.)
Pa:	(Reads the paper.)
Sis:	(Feels mad.)
Pa:	(Feels mad.)

A game can be broken up at any point by either of the persons involved if one of them decides to *do* something differently or *feel* differently than they normally do and feel.

To discover one of your game plans, write down answers to the following questions:

What keeps happening over and over that leaves someone

feeling badly? ______________________________

How does it start? ______________________________

What happens next? ______________________________

How does it end? ______________________________

How does each person feel when it ends? ______________

____

What could each person have done differently that would have changed the game?

"I'm fat because I always eat when I'm rejected."

"I'm leaving, Mr. Benson. Hire yourself a new secretary."

"I'll kill you if you ever do that again."

Some people enter games more seriously than others, and play for higher stakes. Such hard game players are into third-degree games, with the ultimate painful prizes of suicide or homicide. They have saved up their negative feelings for years and feel justified in their actions.

Second-degree game players are going for prizes that involve some kind of withdrawal from a particular situation. These people save up enough bad feelings to feel justified in quitting a job, school, a marriage, or some other important life situation.

First-degree, soft game players are less destructive. They cash in their negative feelings often for small prizes. The prizes they feel justified in collecting are temper tantrums, crying jags, food orgies, drinking sprees, depression blues, and so forth.

Fill in the blanks below to get a clearer idea of what degree games you might be involved in.

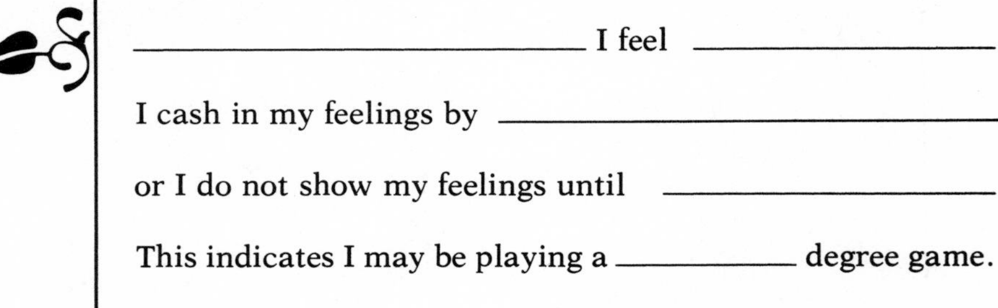

When something negative happens to me such as ____________

______________________________ I feel ____________________.

I cash in my feelings by ______________________________

or I do not show my feelings until ____________________.

This indicates I may be playing a ____________ degree game.

If I did ____________________ instead of saving my negative

feelings, I would ______________________________.

"Let's not get into a big fight over such a small thing."

"I'm not going to leave just because I'm depressed."

"Don't worry. I know it was crazy of me to take all those sleeping pills. I won't do it again."

All people play games. Some people play them continually, some seldom play. Some people play hard games, some play soft games. To de-escalate is to lower the level of game playing, so that games occur less often and with less intensity.

Describe a situation where a third-degree game was being played: ______________________________

Who could have done what to de-escalate the game? ______

____

Describe a situation where a second-degree game was being played: ______________________________

Who could have done what to de-escalate the game? ______

____

"And furthermore, I think clearly, have a good sense of humor, and can be depended on."

"Ah ha! Now I've caught you being supercreative again."

All games start with some kind of "con." In the usual not-OK game, the con ultimately leads to a negative payoff. In contrast, good games[5] are fun and the con leads to positive feelings. Everybody wins and no one loses. Four such games are:

- *Ain't It Wonderful.* Example: Lights go off suddenly, most people complain, except one person who says, "Ain't it wonderful to rest our eyes for a bit."
- *And Furthermore.* Example: Persons unable to accept compliments contract to do so and are to add, *"And furthermore,"* then state three additional good things about themselves.
- *If It Weren't for You.* Example: Students telling a teacher, not with sarcasm but with exaggerated enthusiasm, that all their achievement is due to the teacher.
- *Cops and Robbers.* Example: Being caught or catching someone else performing a desirable act.

Good games are optional. Although people do not need to play them, if they do, the number and intensity of destructive games are decreased. Laughter is a good antidote for many things.

Complaints I recently made or felt like making	*How I could have responded with a good game*
______________________________	______________________________
______________________________	______________________________

"I'm going to give up being a Persecuting Ogre."

"I don't need to act the Victim like the Poor Little Match Girl."

"Actually, I get tired playing the Robin Hood Rescuer role."

If people decide to give up the not-OK games that fit into their destructive or going-nowhere scripts, they must also decide to give up the fairytale or storybook roles they selected when they were children. De-gaming is giving up archaic roles and choosing to be authentic. To de-game is to be real, to live in the here and now, to actually *be* with people, not just do things with them. To be with people is to see them the way they really are, not to see them according to childhood programming. To be with people is to be flexible, to shift ego states at will rather than stay in a favorite one. To be with people is to be capable of intimacy and openness, and to develop these capacities instead of playing games.

Recall a favorite childhood story. Note the different drama roles (Victim, Persecutor, and Rescuer) and how the roles shift. The shift in roles indicates a game. Or, watch a TV drama to observe the games being played there.

Storybook or TV characters	*Roles they played*	*Shift of roles*	*Possible games*
____________	____________	____________	____________
____________	____________	____________	____________
____________	____________	____________	____________

Consider parallels in your life with the characters above.

"What I really *want* is . . ."

"What I really *need* is . . ."

People learn to play games in childhood because they don't know how to get their needs met directly. Yet after a negative game, there is often a positive pay-off for the persons involved. This pay-off is something the person wants or needs. For example, some people fight alot, playing *Uproar,* so that they can then avoid each other and have some time alone. Being alone (behind a book, in a workshop, etc.) is their positive pay-off. Some people overwork, playing *Harried,* until they collapse and get time off with someone to care for them. Being taken care of is their positive pay-off. It's what they want or need.

People who are de-gaming go *directly* for the positive pay-off, rather than *indirectly* through manipulative game playing.[6]

Specify some positive pay-offs you want or need and discover ways to get them directly, without playing a game.

Positive pay-offs I want or need.	*How to be direct to get what I want or need.*	*Self-contract I need to make*	*Interpersonal contracts I need to make*
____________	____________	____________	____________
____________	____________	____________	____________
____________	____________	____________	____________

Contracts I am willing to make to get what I want or

need: ____

Notes

14 Cross-ups and Conflicts

Dealing with cross-ups and conflicts

Crossed transactions are unavoidable in most interpersonal relationships. So are conflicts. Learning how and why cross-ups occur and how and why they *sometimes* lead to conflict is crucial to the new relating self.

Cross-ups sometimes destroy a relationship, sometimes help it grow. Conflicts do the same. Many people become anxious or angry when they are crossed or cross others, or when they are faced with conflict.

It usually takes courage to face cross-ups and conflicts. It also takes planning and creativity to deal successfully with them. They can be ignored, escalated, or "worked through." When they are worked through, the cross-ups and conflicts are resolved.

Cross-ups as crossed transactions

Cross-ups occur when one person "crosses" what the other person *intended* to be a complementary transaction. The cross-up is a crossed transaction because the message sent by one person gets an *unexpected* response from another.

Although, according to Berne, many possible types of crossed transactions can take place,only the four illustrated in our diagram (p. 250) occur frequently in daily life.[1]

Crossed transactions are often related to needs conflicts or value collisions.

Needs conflicts

A need is defined as the lack of something wanted or deemed necessary. The most obvious needs are *physical:* "I'm thirsty," or, "I'm too hot, I need to cool off," or, "I need the car to get to work by 4:30." Needs may also be *psychological:* "I need to know that I am loved," or, "I'm scared and need reassurance," or, "I really need some positive strokes today." Different people seem to have different needs.

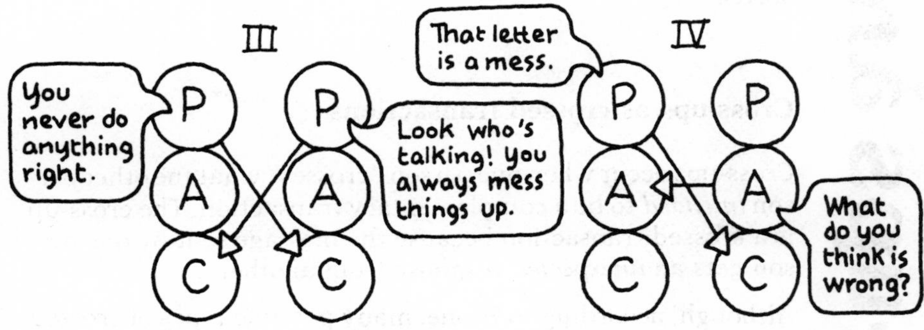

Needs usually may be satisfied by some *object* (a warm coat, a cold drink, a place to sleep, fresh air, a cigarette, etc.) or *action* (a hug, a compliment, some reassurance, a welcome, an invitation, etc.).

In a needs conflict, the people involved have different needs and can usually point to some *concrete and tangible effect* the need is having on them. For example, partners together on a holiday may experience a needs conflict when one needs sleep and says, "I can't keep going without more rest," while the other needs exercise and says, "I'm uptight if I don't use my muscles."

When in a genuine needs conflict, some people are willing to compromise or postpone relieving their needs, since their "relationship" is more important to them than a specific need. Others are not. When compromise is impossible, personal values may be at the heart of the problem.

Value collisions

A value may be defined as *a fundamental personal belief about the meaning and significance of oneself, others, or the world.* Important values and beliefs continually influence a person's thoughts, feelings, attitudes, and behavior.

Certain values, such as security, freedom, salvation, justice, unity, friendship, and so forth, are *major values.* They give a person's life its direction, its character, and its goals.

Other values that directly influence people's daily activity and interaction might be labeled *everyday values.* These include cleanliness, efficiency, orderliness, helpfulness, creativity, affection, promptness, cooperation, attractiveness, etc.

Values are beliefs people verbalize or act out which tend to reveal who they are. Values help to define personal identity, as a religious person might value salvation or a scientist might value truth. Since values are a part of one's self-image, to enter a values collision is to put *oneself* on the line. A values collision also challenges others' fundamental beliefs about themselves and "how things should be." Collisions between people often occur when their values are challenged or threatened.

Relation of values and needs

Values collisions are often related to needs conflicts and sometimes are fused and confused with them. While needs refer to concrete objects or actions, values refer more directly to meanings and beliefs. An interpersonal problem may involve both needs and values.

To decide whether a given conflict is resolvable, it helps to clarify whether only needs are at stake or whether personal values are clearly at stake, too. Usually this question may be answered with Adult analysis of the conflict.

At times, however, people are reluctant to bridge an information gap by clearly expressing their needs. They may be unwilling to take "no" for an answer, or may feel embarrassed to disclose their "need." This may happen if people are hungry, thirsty, bored, late, or when they need a hug, or excitement, or sex, or a trip to the bathroom. They may *value* "keeping their mouth shut" or "keeping personal matters to themselves" more highly than having their needs met.

Needs, values, and games

Needs conflicts and values collisions may lead to destructive psychological games if someone's needs or values are used by someone else as weapons to hurt or threaten. For example, if I respond to your expressed need for sexual experience with ridicule, that's a game. Or, if you reveal how strongly you value cleanliness and order and I immediately point out ("Now I've got you") how often you're sloppy or disorderly, that's a game.

Needs and values may also generate games when people refuse to directly express their needs and instead hint at them, or use some other ulterior transaction that leads to game playing.

Further, people may play games by disguising their needs as values, for example, by intensifying a need into a demand (I *must* have it right now!), or by equating another's refusal to fill one's need with personal rejection ("If you don't lend me ten dollars, I'll know you're really not my friend").

Needs conflicts and values collisions are the critical testing ground of relationships. Resolution of conflicts and collisions is possible between healthy relating selves. People with a history of conflicts that frequently end up in games usually reveal unhealthy relating selves. In any case, no relationship is without its cross-ups and conflicts, and every relating self has ways of dealing with them.

Typical cross-ups

"When you talked about me in public, you crossed me up."

"I feel we often are at cross purposes."

"Sometimes you're direct, other times you're unpredicable."

Sometimes in a relationship, one person may feel crossed up by the other. Crossed transactions occur whenever an unexpected ego-state response follows a given stimulus. For example, a person who initiates a transaction by asking for help, and instead gets criticism, will feel crossed. A person who asks for information and instead gets a whining, "I don't know," will also feel crossed. So, too, a person who offers nurturing help and gets a snarl in return.

Record recent transactions you initiated and whether you were crossed or not.

The situation	*My stimulus*	*The response*	*Crossed or not?*
__________	__________	__________	__________
__________	__________	__________	__________

Now record the reverse — when somebody else initiated the transaction and you responded.

The situation	*Initial stimulus*	*My response*	*Crossed or not?*
__________	__________	__________	__________
__________	__________	__________	__________

"You never listen to me."

"I can't understand you when you whine and cry."

"If you gave me some facts, I would respond differently."

"How about noticing what's going on emotionally in this family instead of just thinking of work?"

One of the interesting skills people can learn is how, when, and why other people respond in noncomplementary ways. Usually it's because the ego state "triggered" is *not* the expected one.

Recall situations in which you felt misunderstood. Which ego state in you felt crossed up? Which ego state in the other person seemed most active? Diagram a few transactions from that situation. Add more series of circles if the transaction continued.

The initial transaction and response

P A C — Me

P A C — Other person

The next transaction

P A C — Me

P A C — Other person

"I'm fed up with trying to please others."

"For years I've tried to adjust to my husband's quirks. Now I'm learning not to give in so easily."

"It's retirement time at last. Now it's *my* time."

People often receive crossed transactions from others because they prefer staying in a particular ego state. Some may feel most comfortable when criticizing or nurturing from their Parent ego state, while others may feel most comfortable when exchanging information from the Adult. Still others may feel most comfortable when complying to other people's expectancies or rebelling against them from the Child ego state. In each pattern of responding, people may claim to be "right" or "doing their own thing," or words to that effect.

Record situations in which you were expected to do something and describe what you actually did. Was this "doing your thing"?

Expected of me	*What I did*	*Did I "do my thing"?*
__________	__________	__________
__________	__________	__________
__________	__________	__________

"I enjoy a good fight. It clears the air."

"I'm scared of fighting or any form of dissension."

"When I experience conflict, I like to work it through and finish it up as quickly as possible."

Conflict with others is an inescapable event in interpersonal relationships, because people have different needs and values that are bound to sometimes clash. Some people relish conflict; they feel it adds drama or melodrama to their lives. Some people avoid it; it is frightening to them and they back off. Other people recognize it as part of being human; they know that conflict can lead to a new self or to a new interpersonal self.

Everyone experiences conflicts. Sometimes these are internal (i.e., between Parent and Child). Sometimes they are interpersonal (i.e., between friends, spouses, family members, etc.). Recall your particular responses to particular conflict situations

A conflict that stimulated me: ______________________

A conflict that scared me: ______________________

A conflict I avoided: ______________________

A conflict I worked through: ______________________

The way I felt after working through a conflict: ________

____

"Let's talk about it tomorrow." (procrastinating)

"Wouldn't you rather watch television?" (distracting)

"Maybe you could blow up the office with dynamite." (humoring)

"Your mother is the one you'll have to talk to about that." (diverting)

"I agree. He is at fault." (agreeing)

"Well, I think you're the best friend anybody could have." (praising)

Many people deal with conflict situations by patterns of avoidance. They usually have been scripted in childhood not to fight, or to be quiet and not to argue, or even not to stick up for their own rights. In the struggle for existence, they have found out that this avoidance behavior works.

Common ways to avoid facing conflicts and problems that need solving include: *procrastinating, distracting, humoring, diverting, agreeing,* and *praising.*[2]

People who use these patterns often avoid working through problems and, consequently, keep having the same kind of difficulties over and over again. By ignoring the feelings of the other people who are involved, they effectively eliminate any chance to get close to them.

People like this often see themselves as lacking courage or without sufficient motivation to change their patterns of avoidance. Thus, they stay in a destructive or going-nowhere script.

(continued)

Consider the six typical avoidance patterns described above. Which of them are especially typical of you? When and with whom do you tend to use these avoidance patterns?

Frequently used	*Seldom used*	*Patterns*	*With whom*
( )	( )	procrastinating	________________
( )	( )	distracting	________________
( )	( )	humoring	________________
( )	( )	diverting	________________
( )	( )	agreeing	________________
( )	( )	praising	________________

These patterns are unhelpful only when used to avoid confronting something in a relationship that needs to be faced. There are many times when humor, praise, agreement, and the rest can significantly foster growth in a relationship.

As you consider your own avoidance patterns, do you need to contract to change any of them?

"You get louder and louder when we disagree."

"You always withdraw into a private world as soon as we begin to differ."

"I'm afraid when you're so blunt."

Some people interact in a low key — their conflicts are seemingly mild and quiet. Others are more outspoken — their conflicts tend to be loud and noisy. The low-key person may save up negative feelings for a long time before exploding or withdrawing, while the intense person's responses are generally more immediate and obvious. The final result, however, is the same.

Recall a situation that started out low key or appeared to be relatively simple and unimportant, but which built up to some kind of explosion. Who said or did what to whom to escalate the conflict?

The situation	*People involved*	*What they did*

Did escalating the conflict solve the problem or not? If not, what could have been said or done that might have been more successful?

"If you won't talk about it now, when would you be willing to do so?"

"Please don't attack me where I'm most vulnerable."

"Let's stick with the problem until it's settled."

Working through conflicts often requires courage, motivation, and a plan. Working through does not mean battling until someone wins and someone loses. In a needs conflict that is worked through, each individual sees and understands the other person's point of view. While this does not always lead to agreement, it often leads to compromise, or to one of the persons changing his or her mind.

Sometimes the worked-through conflict leads to a *decision.* The decision may be to compromise or accommodate in some way, or to stop the battle and avoid the subject in the future. It may be to change the relationship or even to sever it. Whatever the result, the issues are delineated and the opinions and feelings of the people involved are clearly expressed.

When people genuinely work through their conflict, mutual respect, in spite of differences, is a common result.

Recall a conflict, a fight, or a difference of opinion you recently had with someone. Was it worked through or left unfinished?

Issue of disagreement	*Other person's argument*	*My argument*	*Outcome*
___________	___________	___________	___________
___________	___________	___________	___________
___________	___________	___________	___________

"I can't get along without music."

"My body just needs to move around."

"I need to be left alone for awhile."

The needs that occur in relationships are both physical and psychological ones. Abraham Maslow suggests that there are five classes of needs, the most basic being the *physiological needs* — for food, clothing, air, shelter, sexual expression, and so on. The second most basic are *safety needs* — to feel safe, secure, protected, trusting. Among growth needs Maslow lists *belongingness* (being at home, feeling a part of a group, feeling loved), *esteem* (self-esteem and showing esteem towards others) and *self-actualizing needs* (for truth, beauty, justice, play, unity, and the like).[3]

Consider an important relationship — with a close friend, a relative, a co-worker, etc. — and check or fill in the blanks.

	Specific needs I have	*Met or not met*	*In what ways*
Physiological:	________	________	________
Safety:	________	________	________
Belongingness:	________	________	________
Esteem:	________	________	________
Self-actualization:	________	________	________

Now consider the other person's needs.

Recognizing a needs conflict

"I want to go to a movie tonight, but he wants to stay home and watch the football game."

"We both need to use the telephone — and there's only one."

"I need sex tonight and my partner is not in the mood."

Frequently in relationships, an immediate personal need will conflict with another person's current needs. For example, I need to be at one end of town tonight and you need to be at the other end, but we have only one car. This situation is called a *needs conflict.* Such conflicts usually involve crossed transactions.

In a healthy relationship, each person feels free to express his or her need to the other without fear of rejection or put-down. Candid expressions of need are Adult-Adult transactions.

Resolution of a needs conflict may be hindered by an overdominant Parent or Child ego state. For example, needs can be turned into demands by a punishing Parent—"I'm in the mood for a sports show, so that's what we're all going to watch on TV right now." Or, true needs may be clouded up or turned into storms by a not-OK Child — "If you don't play with me, I'm going to take my ball and go home."

Even when two people are in their Adult ego states, conflict may arise because of an information gap, that is, each person may have incomplete or wrong data.

Recall some recent needs conflicts you were a part of. Describe one where the conflict was resolved peacefully and one where the conflict was not resolved. Explain which ego states got in the way.

"My life has been a constant search for truth."

"Honesty is the best policy for me."

"My life centers around fun and play."

"The greatest of all values is love."

Values are different from needs in four ways. First, while needs are often concrete and physical, values are abstract and theoretical. Values are like principles — people are willing to fight for them, cherish them, think of them almost as personal possessions.

Second, while people are willing to compromise their needs, they are very reluctant to budge even an inch when personal values are at stake. Values give essential meaning to one's life.

Third, while needs tend to be specific and immediate, values are more general and permanent, like choosing an overall OK or not-OK life position.[4]

Fourth, while needs have to do with particular things that are wanted, usually here and now, values transcend time and space.

Many people express their values in the form of fundamental beliefs. For example, they might say, "I believe that people should work hard" (hard work is a value). Or, "I believe that people should obey their superiors" (obedience is a value). Or, "I believe that friendship is the most important relationship" (friendship is a value).

Often, values will be translated into positive actions. People who value health will act in health-nourishing ways. People who value beauty will find their way to situations of beauty.

(continued)

What are some of your life values (or fundamental beliefs about life)? How do these values express themselves in your words and actions?

Some of my life values	*How they give meaning to my life*	*How I express my values*

Look back at Chapter 1. Are the values you listed above things you would be willing to live for or die for? Now consider someone who is close to you or important to you.

Some of other person's values	*Meanings the values might have*	*How the person expresses the values*

Are your values harmonious or in conflict with the above person?

Recognizing a values collision

"Enjoying people means more to me than a perfect house."

"I refuse to compromise on the matter of honesty."

"I value your friendship, but I won't live with you because I can't stand the noise in this neighborhood."

"I'm willing to work with you, but not at the expense of my time with my children."

When conflict is about personal values — for example, when the wife feels the *children* are most important and the husband feels the *marriage* is most important — the values collision cannot be resolved in the same way that a needs conflict might be resolved. For, while people can *compromise* over needs, wishes, wants, and the like, they usually refuse to compromise with personal values.

Values are closely linked to meanings. For example, some people habitually share food, money, and opportunities with others. This has a special *meaning* for them because they *value* "equality."

Other persons' habits of saving food, money, and opportunities for themselves have a special meaning to them because they value thriftiness or financial security.

Values may be expressed in any of the three ego states. Things your parents attached importance to (going to church, being thrifty, being educated) that you still value are Parent-centered values. Things you valued when you were young (having your own way, being carefree, being curious) and continue to value are Child-centered values. Things you prize because of experience or study (being accurate, being fair, being effective) are Adult-centered values.

List some of your Parent-centered, Adult-centered, and Child-centered values, and do the same for someone close to you. Then, compare both sets of values and note where conflicts might arise.

(continued)

Recognizing a values collision (continued)

My Parent-centered values	*Another's Parent-centered values*
______________	______________
______________	______________
______________	______________

My Adult-centered values	*Another's Adult-centered values*
______________	______________
______________	______________
______________	______________

My Child-centered values	*Another's Child-centered values*
______________	______________
______________	______________
______________	______________

Can you recall any values collisions that have occurred between you and the other person? Do they relate to your differing values?

"I need to work a lot because I value being productive."

"I need to just wander from time to time because freedom is important to me."

"I need to pray a lot because I value my relationship to God."

Needs conflicts are very different from values collisions, yet needs and values are related. For example, people who value education feel a strong need to go to school or to study, while people who do not value education view school as a waste of their time. Similarly, people who value being in excellent physical condition may feel a strong need to play sports, exercise, and eat nutritious foods, while people who place little value on physical condition may show little interest in such activities.

Because of the close relation between needs and values, a needs conflict can easily and unnecessarily escalate into a large-scale values collision. Conversely, when people seem to be in a values collision, the situation may be reducible to one or more needs conflicts. So, whenever possible, look first for needs conflicts (that are concrete, specific, temporary, and resolvable). Once the needs conflicts are out of the way, values collisions may be recognized and dealt with clearly.

Consider some of your more important Parent-centered, Child-centered, and Adult-centered values. Connected to each *value*, are certain *needs* that you will seem to feel and think of as important.

Check those needs in your list that can easily lead to conflicts with others (or may have already led to conflict). Check also those needs that can be escalated into values collisions with others close to you.

(continued)

Parent value	*Needs related to the value*	*Can lead to conflict*	*Can escalate to value collision*
___	___	___	___
___	___	___	___
___	___	___	___
Adult value			
___	___	___	___
___	___	___	___
___	___	___	___
Child value			
___	___	___	___
___	___	___	___
___	___	___	___

Is there anything you can do about the needs conflicts or value collisions? Do you need to heighten your courage or motivation? Or do you need a plan of action with contracts to enhance your life?

Notes

INFORMATION
INCOMING TRAINS
BULLETIN BOARD
TRACK 42

15 Complementary Relating

Relating in complementary ways

Flexibility and fluidity are marks of a dynamic relationship. Relating people sometimes have needs conflicts and values collisions; however, they work at solving them. Thus, their interpersonal selves continue to grow with ever-expanding new dimensions and their inner-core energies flow freely. They are vivacious people and have lively, living relationships because they use many complementary transactions.

A complementary transaction is sometimes a compliment and sometimes not. A *compliment* is a statement of approval, admiration, or praise. This praise may be genuine, or merely a courteous ritual or piece of flattery.

A *complement* is that which supplies a deficiency. It often implies two things which mutually complete each other and together constitute a whole.

A *complementary transaction* fills out and completes by supplying what is lacking. Thus, if a kindergarten child fears his first day of school and looks to a parent for protection, and the parent meets this need and provides protection and reassurance, the transaction is complementary — the expected response has been given.

There are five basic types of complementary transactions as illustrated in the accompanying diagram.

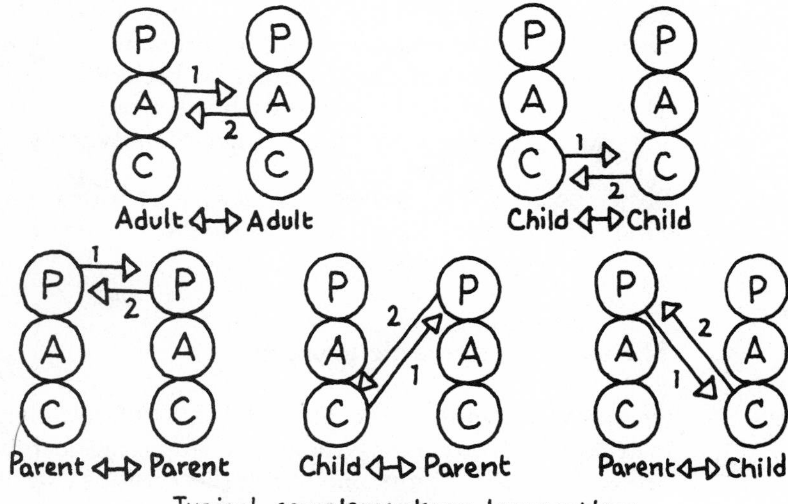

Typical complementary transactions

A common Adult-to-Adult complementary transaction is the exchange of information, while a common Child-to-Child transaction is one person telling a joke and the other person laughing. A Parent-to-Parent complementary transaction might involve commiserating together about "the good old days." From Child-to-Parent, it could take the form of asking for help and getting it; from Parent-to-Child, it could be demanding obedience and getting it.

Complementary transactions are usually the most satisfying ways of transacting. Berne describes a complementary transaction as one which is "appropriate and expected and follows the natural order of healthy human relationship."[1]

In complementary transactions, the lines of communication between the ego states are most often parallel. Communication remains open and the people involved can continue parallel transacting indefinitely.

Static and dynamic relationships

Though complementary transactions are most often helpful, they sometimes block people from growing. When the partners involved *consistently* transact with each other in one particular way and ignore other possibilities for interacting, they are not permitting exploration of other interaction dimensions. In other words, people can get stuck in boring or destructive complementary relationships and may not have the courage, motivation, or a plan for breaking out of them. Thus, their relationship becomes a burden rather than a blessing, the communication static rather than dynamic.

On the positive side, complementary transactions, when used creatively, offer the most direct way to move into healthy intimate relationships.

The static-to-dynamic process

One way to evaluate the pros and cons of complementary transactions is to observe the underlying relationships of the people involved. Complementary relationships can be either static or dynamic.

People in static relationships continually interact in the same habitual ways. They may actually prefer this sameness, viewing their relationship as predictable and, therefore, safe.

Other people prefer dynamic relationships which are fluid, changing, and growing. They enjoy being free to switch ego states when appropriate and they anticipate the richness that develops in the relating self when many kinds of transactions are used.

When relationships move in a healthy direction from static to dynamic, the process seems to involve all, or most, of the following steps:

Static relationship ⟶ Negative feelings ⟶
Crossed transactions ⟶ Conflict ⟶
Resolution or separation

Usually, *static relationships* are first noticed when negative feelings of boredom, resentment, or "being stuck" begin to surface. When locked into one particular type of complementary transaction, the relationship automatically generates dissatisfaction: "We always seem to do the same old things. Nothing new ever happens to us."

Sometimes these feelings are enough to make a person pack up and leave. More often, however, one of the partners is motivated to use *crossed transactions* in the hope of clarifying the problem, improving the relationship, or creating a way of escape.

Conflict is set up as soon as a crossed transaction interrupts the familiar pattern. "Hey, you're not acting the way you always do. What's the matter?" or, "You've got a problem and what are you going to do about it?" Sometimes the conflict *resolves* itself in an agreement to break up the relationship — a rather drastic resolution, but one that may well be the most beneficial to each person's interpersonal self. At other times, the conflict resolves itself in an agreement to improve the relationship by enriching it with a variety of new complementary transactions.

In either case, resolution can break up destructive or going-nowhere scripts, so that those involved can more readily perceive and appreciate the true meaning and value of their relationship.

"When I'm with you, I can just be me."

"You're fun, caring, and interesting to be with."

"I'm glad we don't always do the same old things."

Most people have some friends, relatives, colleagues, or buddies that they especially enjoy being with, usually because the two involved share an abundance of complementary transactions. In such relationships, ulterior games and cross-ups that lead to conflicts are kept to a minimum. Some strong positive relationships are characterized by habitual ways of transacting; others are more fluid.

List some of your favorite people and think about the ways you most often transact with them.

My favorite people	*Our most frequent complementary transactions*	*Our least frequent complementary transactions*
________________	________________	________________
________________	________________	________________
________________	________________	________________

Do you find that you use all ego states with your favorite people or do you transact most often from only one?

"Please do what you're told!" — "All right, all right."

"You never ask me what I think." — "Don't bother me."

"You're always begging me for something." — "I can't help it."

In Parent-to-Child or Child-to-Parent complementary transactions, the one who acts from the Child usually is seen as subordinate to the other.

Those in their Child seek Parent figures to meet their needs. They like to initiate Child-to-Parent transactions.

Those who act from their Parent encourage others to come to them for help and nurturing, or for criticism and censure. They feel comfortable when initiating Parent-to-Child transactions.

While some dependency transactions are appropriate, people who continually transact from dependency positions develop unhealthy relating selves and exclusively symbiotic relationships.

With people who are important to you, do you sometimes experience a dependency relationship — that is, do you feel a need to be dependent on the other person, or to have others dependent on you?

People with whom I have dependency relationships	*How and when I express my childlike dependency*	*How and when I express my parental care toward them*
__________	__________	__________
__________	__________	__________
__________	__________	__________

"I can't do it." — "Well, I'm *always* willing to help you."

"I'm depressed." — "Cheer up. Things are going to be alright."

In dynamic relationships, Child-to-Parent complementary transactions are often appropriate, such as in times of crisis when a person needs comforting, or when a difficult task must be done and parental guidance is needed.

Static Child-to-Parent relationships are limiting, because both persons remain consistently locked into a "favorite" ego state. Usually, one person acts primarily as a helpless (or hostile) Child, while the other acts primarily as a helpful (or critical) Parent.

Watch a popular TV drama where static Child-to-Parent relationships are played out. Are any of these static patterns similar to your own? Then, list some people you relate to consistently in Child-to-Parent patterns, i.e. expecting help, care, or criticism. Do you relate to each of these people in other than Child-to-Parent ways?

People I am Child-to-Parent with	*Other ways we sometimes relate to each other*
______________________	______________________
______________________	______________________
______________________	______________________

"Let's go run on the beach." — "Yeh, let's go!"

"I'd like to get even with the boss." — "I'll help you."

"How about a little loving?" — "I'm for it."

Complementary transactions between the Child ego states in two individuals may relate to physical pleasure or creative, imaginative activities. Or, they may take the form of compliance or rebellion from the Adapted Child.

Child-to-Child transactions that express similar needs, values, or feelings create a strong, binding attraction between people. Some of the most important Child-to-Child ego state experiences happen in childhood between children who are peers, and between children and the grownups who play with them, transacting Child-to-Child.

Recall several of your childhood friends. What feelings, needs, and values did you share? What happened to the bond between you?

Childhood friends (or grownups you used to play with)	*The bond between us was*	*What happened to the bond*
________________	________________	________________
________________	________________	________________
________________	________________	________________

"I caught some trout today up at Clear Lake." — "Is that a good fishing spot?"

"When's quitting time?" — "In about fifteen minutes."

"Have you ever had an acupuncture treatment?" — "No, but I've just read an article on it."

A simple and direct exchange of information and facts is a sign of Adult ego states interacting. So is the recounting and sharing of personal experience, or the exchange of ideas, or coming to a mutual decision.

People interact from their Adult ego states to get in touch with both outer and inner worlds. The Adult gathers information about people, places, things, events, situations, processes, ideas, and their application. The Adult also classifies, categorizes, and processes this information to clarify what is really going on — inside a person as well as outside.

List some people with whom you frequently relate on an Adult-to-Adult basis, and describe some ideas, information, facts, or experiences that reflect complementary transactions.

People I interact with Adult-to-Adult	*Our complementary transactions involve*

"What is, is." — "Yes, that's the truth."

"Children should be seen and not heard." — "I agree."

"Things aren't what they used to be." — "I miss those good old days."

Often when people share similar opinions, lifestyles, and prejudices, it is because they have similar values and needs in their Parent ego states.

Prejudices are preconceived judgments and opinions, which are generally formed without sufficient grounds or knowledge. Prejudices may be viewed as unexamined but firmly held beliefs about the way things are. Many parents, for example, have unexamined but firmly held beliefs about the right and wrong ways to rear children.

Think of someone you know well, preferably someone whose Parent figures you also know, and make note of your Parent responses to the topics in the left column.

	My Parent values, traditions, etc.	*The other person's Parent values, traditions, etc.*	*Are they compatible?*
Money	____________	____________	____________
Work	____________	____________	____________
Family life	____________	____________	____________
Education	____________	____________	____________
Fun	____________	____________	____________

How do you get along when both of you are in your Parent ego states?

"We never seem to do anything but solve *her* problems."

"Our relationship is all work and no play."

"He's only interested in my body."

"I get tired of talking to a 'computer' all the time."

Relationships built on a single constant type of complementary transaction eventually become boring to the people involved — they may feel "stuck" in the relationship. Frequently, too, resentment builds up, along with anger and frustration. Sometimes the person who feels stuck blames the other person for their dissatisfaction — e.g., "If it weren't for you, we could be having a good time today," or, "That's all you *ever* want to do."

Do any of your important relationships — at home, at work, or among friends — seem stuck with a single constant type of complementary transaction? If so, with whom?

What constant transaction do the two of you use?

What negative feelings tend to surface in you when you are with this person or when you think about your relationship?

What do you usually do about them?

"I'm sick and tired of talking about physics. Let's go for a ride in the country."

"I've just realized that you never want to go anywhere unless I come along. Do you observe that to be true?"

"We've been playing for an hour. Would you like to spend an hour going over the new contracts?"

☙

Static relations often lead to negative feelings and boredom. If partners wish to change the situation, they may use crossed transactions to do so. In such cases, crossed transactions are often healthy and effective.

The process is simple. First, clarify the type of complementary transaction into which you and your partner are locked. Second, change your own ego state. And third, speak *from* a different ego state *to* a different ego state in your partner. For example, if your relationship has been Parent to Child, then try being in your Adult and addressing your partner's Adult. Or, if your pattern has been Adult to Adult, try initiating a Child-to-Child exchange.

Using a crossed transaction may clarify the problem without resolving it, but at least it brings the situation into sharper focus by interrupting the static pattern. Unless one or the other partner decides to change the pattern, the relationship is not likely to improve.

☙

Think of a relationship in which you might be stuck, or a static relationship you have observed. Discover the constant transactional pattern being used.

Describe some ways that changing ego states, in order to cross the pattern, might clarify the problem.

"When people bore me, I just say goodbye."

"If we broke up, it would shatter me emotionally."

"How can I leave her after all these years?"

"Just thinking about breaking up helped me realize how important the relationship is to me."

Sometimes the only way to relieve a static relationship is to leave it. Some people prefer to come unstuck gradually; others prefer to break apart rapidly.

Breaking up is easy, for example, when people place little value on their partnership and simply drift apart. At other times, however, breaking up is extremely difficult. When people's values include loyalty and fidelity to promises they made, such as in marriage, getting unstuck is an agonizing process. Feelings of guilt or depression frequently accompany the very thought of a break. The people involved may also find themselves unable to make routine decisions and unable to carry out decisions they do make.

Is there a static relationship in your life in which you feel stuck? Why do you think you can't get out of it? ________

What are your reactions when you think about breaking up the relationship? Specify for each ego state:

Parent reaction	*Adult reaction*	*Child reaction*
________	________	________

How are your needs and values involved in this relationship?

____

From static to dynamic

"There *must* be hope for our friendship."

"I'd like to save our marriage, if we can."

"It may be difficult, but let's try to be different."

For many static relationships, breaking up is inappropriate and unnecessary. More desirable is transforming the static relationship into a dynamic one. The process requires the cooperation of both parties, and may be facilitated by a series of clear and practical interpersonal contracts.

The procedure is simple in theory, but takes courage, motivation, and planning to carry out. In theory, making a relationship dynamic involves using a variety of complementary transactions. For example, if the relationship has been locked into Parent-to-Child transactions, the people involved will need to contract to try periods of Adult-to-Adult, Child-to-Child, and so on.

Note that while you were asked to use *crossed transactions* to *clarify* the static relationship, you are being asked to develop new kinds of *complementary transactions* to inject *dynamism* into the relationship.

Is there a relationship in your life that you would like to make more dynamic? If so, with whom? ______________________

Note the types of complementary transactions that are most common in your relationship now, and which kinds seem to be weakest.

	Often use	*Rarely use*
Adult-to-Adult	( )	( )
Child-to-Child	( )	( )
Parent-to-Parent	( )	( )
Child-to-Parent	( )	( )
Parent-to-Child	( )	( )

You may decide to make an interpersonal contract to add to your relationship those transactions you use most infrequently.

Meaning in complementary transactions

"I'm tired of being your doll-baby wife. It's lost its meaning."

"Thinking things through with you has great meaning for me."

"When we play and laugh together, I feel life makes sense."

In Chapter 1 we noted that people tend to find meanings in three areas of their lives — in tasks, in positive experiences and feelings, and sometimes in unavoidable suffering — one's own or someone else's.

These meanings may be experienced on an individual basis or at an interpersonal level where the tasks, experiences, and suffering are shared. Sharing often generates many complementary transactions.

Consider some areas where you and someone else have experienced meanings together. Make a *rough* guess at the percentage of complementary transactions that were involved.

Areas of meaning	*Meanings for the relating self*	*Percentage of complementary transactions*
Shared tasks	________________	________________
Shared experiences	________________	________________
Shared suffering	________________	________________

Notes

16 Using Time

The changing uses of time

During America's pioneer days, people's lives revolved around their work. Lacking the luxuries that are available to us today, almost everyone, including children, had to toil long hours just to survive. Life expectancy was a mere forty years. Their hand-to-mouth existence required a dawn-to-dark working schedule, with little time for leisure.

With industrialization and automation, leisure time increased and the middle years were seen in a new light. The 1930s best-seller, *Life Begins at Forty,* is indicative of this change. Being forty had a glamour ring to it — except to those young people who claimed not to trust anyone over thirty.

For most people today, retirement is mandatory between ages sixty-two and sixty-five, and currently the national life expectancy is seventy-eight. Age fifty-five will admit a person into a swank retirement community.

Today, however, many older people are refusing to conform to the rocking-chair routine. Instead, they continue their hobbies or professions, or they begin exciting new careers and develop new interests. Their plan is to go on living into their nineties by playing, loving, and working, because they have discovered these activities give meaning to life. In a way, they are giving a new meaning to time.

Clock time and meaningful time

The early Greeks and Hebrews conceptualized time in an interesting way. Although they acknowledged *clock time* (chronos), what was more important to them was *meaning-filled time* (kairos). Hours, days, months, or years were not their focus of interest. Rather, the *event*, and the *meaning of the event* were important. An event-filled time was an opportune time which called forth a response. The *challenge* of the event and the response it evoked gave meaning to time.[1]

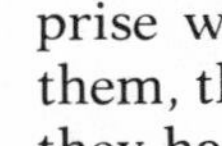

Most people have, at one time or another, experienced surprise when the clock has told them, "It's time to go." For them, the situation and event had become so meaningful that they had moved outside of linear time, into another time dimension.

Although many people have had this experience of time flying by, most people have also experienced time *dragging*. They have looked at their watches again and again, wondering why its hands were moving so slowly. The situation and event they were in apparently had little or no meaning for them.

From cradle to grave, the question of what to do in the time available to us is a most basic one. Time management specialists are becoming increasingly popular, especially in business firms, and they don't simply "watch the clock."

Body time

The human body seems to have its own built-in clock, which works on different cycles. Certain body patterns, such as breathing and heartbeat, operate on very short cycles; other cycles, such as hunger and eating, thirst and drinking, work and rest, take a certain number of hours to come full circle. Daily cycles of sleeping and waking are most obvious. And, although monthly cycles are clearest in women's bodies, recent research indicates that everyone experiences monthly periods of high energy and low energy, high creativity and low.

The body's clock tells a person when to slow down, when to take a break, and when the body is unwell and needs to heal or recuperate. Over one's lifetime, it signals the passage of youth, the prime of life, and the onset of old age.

It takes courage at times to face your own body clock, especially when its message is that you are growing older or that you are harming your body in some way. Sometimes, only a serious illness is sufficient motivation to get a person to heed their body's messages.

Even in relating to others, the body clock communicates messages, such as, "I feel uncomfortable when I blush like this," or, "This relationship is putting too much stress on me," or, "I need some physical activity to counteract the boredom."

Time structuring

Managing your own time — clock time, meaningful time, and body time — is important in developing an effective relating self.

According to TA, people structure their time with other people in six ways: *psychological withdrawal, rituals, pastimes, games, activities,* and *intimacy.* Actually, it is often during activities that the other forms of time structuring occur.

Two people might be working together on a project (activity) and one or both might daydream about being somewhere else (psychological withdrawal), or they might greet each other with stereotyped transactions (ritual), or chat informally about sports, family, etc. (pastime), or get involved in an argument (often, though not always, a game), or experience closeness, openness, and trust (intimacy).

Each form of time structuring may be *used* to enhance living, or *abused*, and thus decrease the joy of existence.

"You never listen when I tell you something."

"I guess I was daydreaming when you were talking."

When people physically withdraw from others, they may do so out of *necessity* (to go to work) or out of *choice* (to be with someone else, or to be alone to think or rest, etc.).

When people withdraw from others psychologically, they are physically but not emotionally present. They may be fantasizing, daydreaming, sulking, wallowing in self pity, or planning a project. They may nod when the other person speaks, even answer in a desultory manner without really hearing what is being said.

Get in touch with your patterns of psychological withdrawal by keeping a one-day diary. Jot down situations in which you find yourself not listening.

The person talking	*Subject being discussed*	*What I was doing in my head*
________________	________________	________________
________________	________________	________________
________________	________________	________________

Would anything be different if you had not withdrawn psychologically?

"Children should stand when elders enter the room."

"Don't forget to say, 'Thank you.' "

Rituals are stereotyped transactions, predictable exchanges of words and behavior, culturally shaped and frequently used. A typical greeting and response: "Hello" — "Hello" is a common two-stroke ritual, often followed by another ritual: "How are you?" — "Fine."

Rituals are commonly accepted ways to initiate contact with others; people who don't use them are often accused of having "bad manners."

However, rituals can be misused. People who maintain their relationships primarily at the ritual level — being overly polite, overly nice, excessively accommodating — are missing the depths of interaction that are possible between two people.

Describe some predictable rituals followed in your family that have to do with:

Greeting and saying good-bye ______________________

Eating meals ______________________

Religious holidays ______________________

Do you know families whose rituals differ from those of your family? Do you tend to misuse rituals by *not using them* when they might be helpful, or by *overusing them* to avoid confrontation or relating at a deeper level?

"She just chatters on and on, and doesn't really *say* anything."

"He could sit and talk sports all day every day if he had the chance."

"Frankly, I get bored with the superficial talk that goes on at cocktail parties."

Pastimes are semiritualistic topical conversations, less predictable and stereotyped than rituals. They are a popular, useful way of structuring time, and a way that can also be abused. Pastimes often naturally follow a greeting ritual and involve exchanges, often at a superficial level, about "safe" subjects — the weather, cars, sports, family, health, bills, television, food, etc.

Pastimes provide a convenient way for people to get better acquainted and to continue making contact. The sequence of pastime conversation is prescribed and circumscribed by certain unspoken but commonly accepted rules. These rules are programmed by society.

When you sit around and pass the time in conversation, what are your favorite topics? List at least five and rank them in order of preference. After each topic, write the names of two or three people with whom you share this pastime.

My favorite pastime topics	*People I share this topic with*

"He usually does things at the last minute, like slamming on the brakes, so that I nearly bump my head on the dashboard."

"She always rushes around like a chicken with its head cut off, and she knows that it makes me hypernervous."

Although a previous chapter was devoted to psychological games *as a way of relating,* it is important also to view games *as a way of spending time.* Berne feels that "the bulk of social activity consists of playing games."[2]

Destructive psychological games are played at various levels of intensity, with a negative pay-off as small as a crying jag or as big as a suicide or homocide. Although many games lead to bad feelings, a small-sized game is less destructive than a game played by someone in for the kill. Yet all such games are a waste of time!

Recall a time spent with others (or another) from which you came away *feeling badly.* (This is usually a sign that a game was being played and you were involved, even though you may have said little or nothing.) Tally up the time consumed in the actual game playing and in dealing later with the negative feelings.

Describe the incident and the people who were present:

____

How much time was spent in the interactions? __________

How long did you harbor these feelings of yourself and/or the other people involved? ____________________

"Let's get to work."

"All you want to do is work, work, work."

"Why play when work is so much fun?"

"He always works overtime just to get away from the kids."

People reared under the Puritan ethic of working hard are often productive and attracted to others who focus their lives around productivity and achievement. Sometimes working is an appropriate activity; sometimes it is a real abuse of time. For example, if a commitment is made to finish a project by a certain time, then it is usually appropriate to do so. However, if finishing the project means working almost around the clock to the detriment of the person's physical health and the emotional well-being of others, then such time is abused.

Recall times when you had tasks that had to be completed by a certain date. Describe the physical and psychological effects of each task on you and others involved.

Situation and task	*Other people involved*	*Task's effect on you*	*Task's effect on them*
________	________	________	________
________	________	________	________
________	________	________	________

"I feel separated when we're in a crowd of strangers."

"I like our times together, just being close."

"Let's take time to go camping alone."

An intimate transaction may occupy only a brief period of time, yet be a moment filled with meaning. On the other hand, transacting intimately may involve a life-long commitment which is also filled with significant meaning. When the latter is the case, other ways of structuring time (rituals, pastimes, etc.) occur periodically. Yet, basically, those who are relating in long-term intimacy are relatively free of games.

List the people in your past, present, or future with whom you have transacted, or hope to transact intimately.

People I have been intimate with	*Ways we spent time*
________________	____________________________
________________	____________________________
People I am intimate with now	*Ways we spend time*
________________	____________________________
________________	____________________________
People I hope to be intimate with	*How we might spend time together*
________________	____________________________
________________	____________________________

"A stitch in time saves nine."

"You know you have to do your chores before you play."

"Go slow, you'll last longer."

"Hurry up, don't be so lazy."

Often, a person's needs are denied or repressed because family or cultural values discourage expression of them. For example, the belief that leisure time *must* be productive is a value held by many parents. Therefore, they may accuse children who are tired, ill, or bored, of being "lazy." "Get to work," is an often-heard parental phrase that scripts children to use their time by working. If children comply, they will work or overwork. If they rebel, they may do so openly by refusing to work, or covertly by procrastinating.

"Don't bother, I'll finish it," is a parental expression that may eventually script a child to leave tasks unfinished, regardless of how much time is allowed. "You can do it if you take time to figure it out," is a healthier kind of message.

Sit down, get comfortable, and take a trip into your past, letting the parental messages you heard on the use of time come into your awareness.

What my parent figures said to me about the use of time	*The message behind their words*	*How they used their own time*
________________	________________	________________
________________	________________	________________
________________	________________	________________

"What isn't worth doing at all is not worth doing well."

"If I list what I need to do and organize according to priorities, I'll finish what's important."

Often, problems can be solved by learning how to manage one's time more effectively. Some people keep lists of things to do and assign priorities to the tasks; others are at a loss when it comes to time management. The basic question to ask oneself is, "What is the best use of my time now?"[3]

The best use of time needs to be related to both general and specific goals.

Without pausing, quickly make a list of your lifetime interpersonal goals. Include as many goals as possible, no matter how impractical or crazy they seem. Then, use your Adult to do some time management.

Interpersonal goals	*Target dates for completing goals*	*What I need to do now to foster the goals*	*How much time would it require?*

"Ugh, what a boring time I had at that party."

"Wow, I had a great time!"

"Gee, I was all the time wishing I was somewhere else."

All children enjoy bodily pleasure, laughter, and play. They are curious, intuitive, and creative, and will use these capacities in a balanced way unless they are adapted somehow to "turn off" these instincts. For example, people who in childhood are trained to work hard and not enjoy life are likely to feel uncomfortable at parties or when they have unstructured time to fill.

Think back to some of the ways you were trained and adapted to use your time. As the ages listed below are arbitrary, select years that you recall the clearest.

	How I was supposed to use my time	*How I wanted to use my time*	*How I actually used my time*
Age 6	______	______	______
	______	______	______
Age 10	______	______	______
	______	______	______
Age 15	______	______	______
	______	______	______

Does a pattern for using time seem to emerge that feels familiar to you currently?

"My job is a waste of time."

"I kill a lot of time at work."

"Time flies when I'm at the office."

☙

Some people think of their jobs as hard work, but necessary for earning a living; others view their workdays as hours for merely "marking time" or "putting in time," as though they were "doing time" in a prison. Still others describe their jobs as enjoyable, stimulating, even fun.

Time can be abused or put to good use. Some people abuse their time by remaining in boring jobs, characteristic of banal, going-nowhere scripts. Others almost kill themselves (or others) by working to exhaustion, typical of destructive scripts. Still others find work exciting and interesting; they look forward to their workday, yet they can also just as eagerly look forward to being with others after work is over. Their scripts are more likely to be winning, constructive scripts.

☙

List some of the words that describe your feelings toward the work you normally do from day to day. About how many hours or minutes per day do you spend feeling this way?

Feelings	*Time spent with feelings*
______________________	______________________
______________________	______________________
______________________	______________________

How would you describe the script you follow during your workday? Constructive? Destructive? Going nowhere?

"All day I've been fantasizing about tonight in bed with you."

"Our sex is the standard variety — nothing new ever happens."

"I need time alone with you before I turn on."

Sexual expression can be healing, exciting, and life-enhancing or a routine procedure which may reduce tension yet have little meaning. Berne writes:

> Sexual activities offer examples which cover this whole spectrum of social behavior. It is evident that they can take place in withdrawal, that they can be part of a ritualistic ceremony, or that they can be all in a day's work, a pastime for a rainy day, a game of mutual exploitation, or acts of real intimacy.[4]

Describe sexual experiences, your own or others', which fit into one or another of the six ways of structuring time.

Structure	*My own or others' sexual experiences*
Withdrawal	________________________
Ritual	________________________
Activities (work)	________________________
Pastime	________________________
Game playing	________________________
Intimacy	________________________

What this means to me is ______________________________

"You're always so tired when you're with me."

"I'm too busy for you now. Make it later."

"I'm saving some energy so we can have a great time when we go out together."

"Leftovers" from the refrigerator may be delectable morsels — or unappetizing remains that have lost their tastiness and freshness. In relationships, leftover time seldom satisfies. Yet, it may be all that one person has to offer another after an exhausting day. In such cases, time in relationship with others may seem flat and tasteless.

In contrast, *prime time,* that is, when persons are alert, interested, and fully present to the relationship, is treasured time. To share your prime time with someone is to give him or her a strong positive stroke. It implies that you value that person and your relationship highly.

Make note of the people who usually experience you in your prime time. Also, note some people who experience you often in leftover time.

My prime time is with	*My leftover time is with*
____________________	____________________
____________________	____________________
____________________	____________________

I sometimes justify giving leftover time to someone by

saying to myself: ______________________________

"I never have any time for myself."

"All my time is spent caring for the children."

"Now that my children are grown up, my time seems so empty."

People sometimes spend all of their prime time with others and have none left for themselves. For example, caring for children often seems like a twenty-four-hour-a-day job that makes impossible demands. People who have jobs that keep them busy all day, every day, also feel deprived of privacy and personal time.

Those who have little or no time for themselves usually receive personal warning signals from their body clocks. Such warnings may take the form of irritability, listlessness, resentfulness, anxiety, loneliness, fatigue, or boredom. Some people never heed these warnings until serious illness strikes and, in effect, forces them to take time for themselves.

What are some of the uses to which you put (or would put) the time that you have for yourself. Note which uses receive your prime time and which receive your leftover time.

Ways I use time for myself	*Prime or leftover time*
____________	____________
____________	____________
____________	____________

How would you describe "the time of your life"?

____

Notes

17 Third-Self Intimacy

Transactions and intimacy

Intimacy is one of the most desirable and desired ways of structuring time. Most people will go to great lengths just to share a moment of genuine intimacy with a friend, for such moments of closeness give life a special meaning.

It takes *courage* to open oneself to the risks of intimacy, and time and careful *planning* to nurture this slow-growing and delicate plant. It also takes *motivation,* for intimacy requires practice in transacting openly.

Giving up destructive game patterns, or turning them into good games which are fun to play, often leads to intimacy.

Similarly, cross-ups and conflicts, when resolved effectively, can lead to interpersonal growth and greater mutual appreciation.

Complementary transactions, when used to transform static relationships into dynamic ones, generally promote increased intimacy.

Life positions, stroking, and intimacy

Self-actualizing, intimate relationships are seldom possible for people whose life positions are fundamentally "superior" (I'm OK — You're not OK), or "hopeless" (I'm not OK — You're not OK), or "anxious" (I'm not OK — You're OK). The mutual acceptance and the sense of equality required in intimacy seem to be lacking in such people.

Intimacy's fullest expression is most open to "confident" people, those whose life positions are I'm OK — You're OK.

Positive stroking fosters and supports OKness in people. It also nurtures mutual acceptance and a sense of equality, the healthy milieu in which intimate relationships can grow in breadth and depth. Once this acceptance is achieved, people who relate are able to clarify interpersonal needs and values and make decisions together.

Acceptance

People engaged in intimacy are vulnerable; consequently, many persons prefer to use pastimes or play games or work side by side rather than risk the face-to-face acceptance or rejection intimacy may involve.

Achieving mutual acceptance — of oneself and of the other person — is the crucial element in intimacy. This acceptance involves admitting or receiving persons into your life exactly as they are at the present moment. The accepting person says, in effect, "It's all right for you to be the way you are right now, and to feel the way you do right now."

Acceptance is a "meeting" — person to person — recognizing the inner-core potentials, not focusing on behavior. When people are accepting, they give many unconditional strokes. Statements such as, "I won't deal with you 'til you've gotten rid of your problem," are replaced by, "It's all right for you to have whatever problem you have. I don't reject you for having a problem."

Acceptance does not make demands. It does not say, "I want you to change." Rather, it asserts, "I don't demand that you change. Whether or not you change is up to you."

"Approval" and acceptance are not synonymous. I may not *approve* of your present problem any more than you do, but I can still clearly show acceptance by saying, "I receive you as someone who happens to have a problem right now."

Nonacceptance

Many people unwittingly communicate nonacceptance to even their closest friends. They say, in effect, "I won't accept you until you change," or, "I want you to be different from what you are right now," or, "I want you to stop having whatever problem you're having." People who show nonacceptance and are aware of it need to get in touch with their current interpersonal language, to see its weaknesses and strengths, as a way of planning for intimacy.

In TA language, nonacceptance translates to, "You're not OK now," or, "You're OK only on the condition that . . . ," and may be expressed from any of the three ego states.

The Parent ego state may evaluate, judge, command, criticize, or direct the other person instead of demonstrating acceptance of them.

The Adult ego state may miss recognizing a person's need for acceptance. Instead, the Adult may immediately begin offering solutions and suggestions toward solving a problem, without fully acknowledging the *person* and their *feelings* (possibly not-OK feelings).

The Child ego state may show nonacceptance quietly and politely by avoidance and distraction, or noisily by getting upset, angry, or hurt.

These nonacceptance patterns may be so habitual that learning mutual acceptance responses feels like learning to speak a new language. The attitude of acceptance is an important part of any intimate relationship. Without acceptance, intimacy is seldom possible.

Formulas for relating

Most relationships may be described by one of four formulas for relating, following a kind of "relationship mathematics."

The first attitude is characteristic of relationships in which *the partners feel incomplete* (only half-persons) unless, like Romeo and Juliet, they are united with their other halves. Or, mathematically:

$$\tfrac{1}{2} \text{ person} + \tfrac{1}{2} \text{ person} \longrightarrow 1 \text{ person}$$

The second relating attitude happens when *one person feels whole and independent but the other feels incomplete and dependent* (only half a person), as a parent relating to a young child. Or, mathematically:

$$1 \text{ person} + \tfrac{1}{2} \text{ person} \longrightarrow 1\tfrac{1}{2} \text{ person}$$

Partners in the third attitude feel that a relationship is not meant to melt people together (as in the first attitude), but to enhance and enrich each person, so that in the end there are still *two unique individuals relating freely and independently.* Or, mathematically,

1 person + 1 person ⟶ 1 person + 1 person

According to the fourth attitude, the relationship between two intimates is sometimes so powerful and dynamic that *the relationship itself can be viewed as a new self.* The partners maintain not only their fullest individuality, but experience a *new personal reality* in the process. There are really three "selves" in the relationship: you, me, and our relationship. The relationship, with a life of its own, becomes what we call a "third self."[1]

Symbolically, this relating process might be represented:

1 person + 1 person ⟶ 1 person + 1 person + a third self

Thus, a process which begins with two persons relating eventually may generate a third self. This third self (the relationship) has its own personality and "ego states." It is *transpersonal* and transcends age, sex, race, and so forth. The third self has its own needs, independent of the needs of the two relating partners. It may be diagrammed:

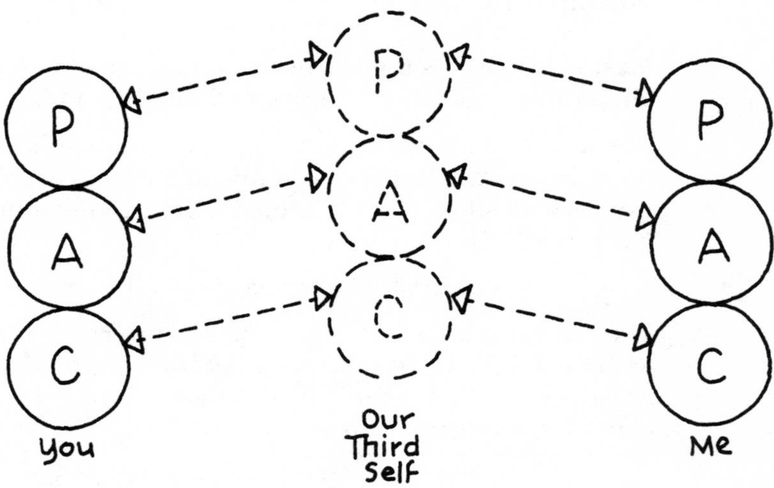

The relationship of intimacy

Caring for this third self is one of the challenges of an intimate relationship.

Intimacy is not merely a matter of healthy transactions among ego states. Intimacy affects people at the inner core level.

Core-to-core intimates are accustomed to sharing their personal thoughts and feelings, their worries and concerns, their interests and experiences, their values and meanings. In their relationships, strong emotions are often felt. Bonds of tenderness and empathy are forged. Genuine caring is present. Energies and enthusiasms seem to flow from one person to the other. Mutual acceptance creates the atmosphere of their third self.

"He has wanted me to be his close friend for years."

"Somehow I can't see myself as an intimate of hers."

"This has been the deepest, most satisfying relationship I could ever have imagined."

Eric Berne defines intimacy as "a candid game-free relationship, with mutual free giving and receiving and without exploitation."[2]

Of course, intimacy cannot develop when one person is open and freely sharing, while the other is devious and exploitative. Accepting intimacy involves becoming vulnerable to another person in certain ways. Sometimes invitations to intimacy are rejected, sometimes they are accepted.

Think back over the past several years and list some of the people who have invited (or are inviting) you into some degree of intimacy. Have you accepted or refused their invitations?

Then list some of the people whom you may have invited (or are inviting) into intimacy. Which of these have accepted or refused your invitation?

People who invite(d) me	*Accepted or refused*	*Reasons I used for accepting or refusing*
____________	______	____________
____________	______	____________

People I've invited into intimacy with me	*Accepted or rejected*	*Reasons they used*
____________	______	____________
____________	______	____________

Conditional OKness

"His constant bragging turns me off."

"If he were more attractive, I think I could get to like him."

"My spouse is OK, except when her mother comes to our house."

"I love her, but she talks too much."

Frequently, people think they are fully accepting another person when they are really saying, "You're OK *only on the condition. . . .*" Conditional OKness is usually based on words, actions, or personal problems of others that we don't like.

Conditions placed on acceptance may force people out of intimacy and into game playing and other devious and exploitative ways of relating. It is helpful to be aware of the ways people condition their OK relationships.

List the names of people with whom you share intimacy at some time or other. After each name, note those words or actions or problems in the other person that can effectively destroy a moment of intimacy for you.

My intimacy sharers	*How our intimacy fades*
____________________	____________________
____________________	____________________
____________________	____________________
____________________	____________________

"I could never love a person like him."

"She's too emotional for me."

"I like her, despite her problems."

"She's growing, and I'm willing to be friends while she grows."

Fundamental to intimacy is *acceptance of the other person as is.* In TA language, this involves the mutual affirmation "I'm OK — You're OK." To say "You're OK" means I recognize and treat you as someone who is capable of living and thinking within an OK life position. I regard you as a unique and important human, and I find meaning and value in you. Even if you have problems, I accept you in the process of dealing with them. Even if you have a long way to grow, I accept you as you are. I say it's OK for you *to be where you are and to be the way you are,* since being-OK itself is a process.

Consider one (or more) of the people with whom you share (or plan to share) intimacy. Describe how you view each one's OKness, in terms of their three ego state qualities.

Name	*Their OK Parent*	*Their OK Adult*	*Their OK Child*
____________	____________	____________	____________
____________	____________	____________	____________
____________	____________	____________	____________

Are there any areas of their lives that you find difficult to accept? If so, how might these hinder your intimacy?

"Who could love me with my looks?"

"I like living inside my skin!"

"I'm a person who's learned a lot from my mistakes."

"Just watch me grow!"

Although it's possible for people who adopt the "I'm not OK" life position to achieve some degree of intimacy, a bilateral intimate relationship seems richest when both partners operate from an OK position.

Saying "I'm OK" involves *accepting myself as is,* that is, *as I am in process.* It means that I feel worthwhile and significant in the world. It means I accept myself as a human with problems, as someone who may still have a lot of psychological and spiritual growing to do, as someone who has failed and made mistakes but who still keeps going. Saying "I'm OK" also means that I see myself bringing unique meaning and value to the relationships I'm part of.

What are some things about yourself that might keep you from seeing yourself as OK? What are some things that could strengthen your belief in your OKness.

What keeps me from fullest OKness	*What strengthens my OKness*
____________________	____________________
____________________	____________________
____________________	____________________

What are some ways you can use to put the balance even more favorably on the side of "I'm OK"-ness?

Intimate stroking

"I felt a renewed sense of trust when you told me about her."

"I feel uneasy when I don't know where you are at night."

"I'm happy when we're together."

"I was disappointed when you called to say you couldn't come."

Although everyone enjoys receiving strokes in general, the most special strokes are ones received from intimates.

Contrary to popular belief, giving evaluative compliments and praise is *not* the most effective way of stroking in an intimate relationship. Even the closest of friends, however, tend to stroke each other in this way. While evaluative strokes may be *positive* ("You're good, beautiful, terrific, nice, fantastic, sweet, intelligent, etc."), they may also be *negative* ("You're bad, stupid, absurd, thoughtless, clumsy, etc.").

The reason evaluative strokes do not usually enrich intimacy is because an evaluation implies that the one who makes the judgment is somehow outside and above the relationship — that is, in a position to judge objectively. Such implied detachment is destructive to intimacy.

Much more effective in promoting intimacy is to describe how you feel in the situation. Instead of saying, "You're a good back-scratcher," try describing — for example, "I tingle all over when you scratch my back."

Descriptive strokes — describing how you feel — keep the judgmental (approving or disapproving) Parent ego state out of the relationship. They evoke the creative OK Child in the other person and feed clear information to the Adult to process and use in the future.

Recall situations with intimates when you used evaluative strokes. Write them down. Then, create an alternative descriptive stroke.

Intimate stroking (continued)

Intimate involved	*Evaluative strokes I used*	*Alternate descriptive strokes I could use*

Then consider the reverse — the evaluative strokes given by intimates and the strokes that describe their feelings which they could have used.

Intimates involved	*Evaluative strokes they used*	*Alternate descriptive strokes they could use*

"Our relationship opens up a new world to me."

"I become a different person when I'm with her."

"What a delight to be together!"

"I like to be with you. You bring out the Child in me."

In certain cases, an intimate relationship becomes so strong that the relationship itself takes on the character of a new, or "third," self. Though dependent on the friends who relate, the third-self relationship seems to enjoy a life of its own. Its birth date is different from the birthdates of the friends who relate; it may die before either of the friends dies, or live beyond the death of one. It may grow strong or weaken independently of either friend, and so on.

When such a third-self relationship is examined separately, the third self also seems to possess a set of ego states, as does each person in the relationship. Its Parent contains the traditions and expectancies for living that the friends follow when relating together. Its Adult contains the information, facts, and experiences that are shared. And its Child expresses the current of feelings — warm, exciting, sexy, joyful, sad — that flow between them.

Do you enjoy some third-self relationships? If so, make note of ways you think, feel, and behave *in the relationships* which are different from the ways you ordinarily do.

Ways I usually am with others	*Ways I am in the third-self relationship*
______________________	______________________
______________________	______________________

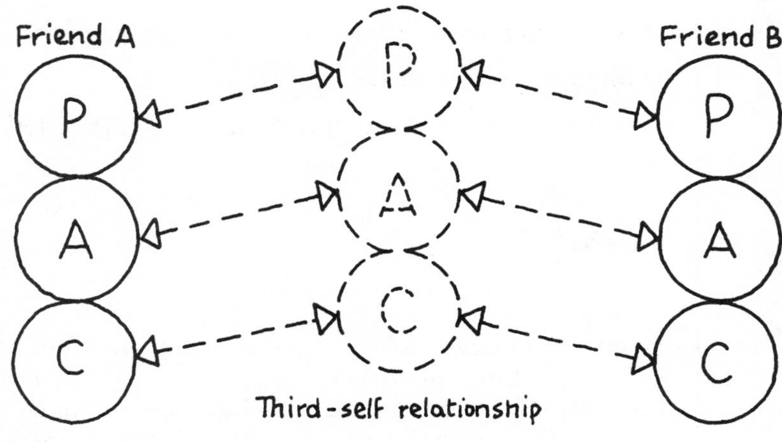

If I wanted *more* third-self relationships, I would need to __________, instead of __________, which I now do. If I have no third-self relationships and want them, I will need to contract to ________________ and be willing to do ________________.

"I get discouraged easily, and I don't like that."

"I'm an inveterate talker, so beware."

"If you can be friends with a Mister Tardy, then let's be friends."

People sometimes take it for granted that what they say or do in relationships has little or no effect on the depth of their intimacy. Yet words and actions significantly shape the third self, keep it healthy, account for its direction of growth, and so on. The third self is created and sustained by the people who relate.

It's usually easy to burden the third self (the relationship) with personal problems, feelings, words, or actions that individuals find unacceptable in themselves. When this happens, the third self suffers, and intimacy becomes increasingly difficult to achieve and maintain.

It is helpful for individuals to realize what feelings, words, actions, and problems they bring to a relationship, and acknowledge ownership of them and responsibility for them.

What are some of the ways you talk or act in relationships that you don't like? ______________________________

____

What are some of the ways you talk or act in relationships that successfully foster intimacy? ______________________________

____

"Hey, my Child is dying from lack of use."

"I don't have very much energy left."

"I need some emotional support this week."

"Being organized is a big value for me."

Being assertive does not necessarily mean being aggressive. In intimacy, each approach has its proper time.

If a third self is to live and grow, both partners need to live and grow, too. Personal needs, preferences, wishes, and values of the partners — as well as those of the third self — all fall into an area where assertiveness is sometimes called for. To defer continually in favor of the other person may, in the long run, destroy the relationship.

When ego states need exercise and expression, or when inner-core energies are blocked or constricted, intimacy calls for assertiveness.

Assertiveness is characterized by "I" expressions, such as "I need . . . ," or "I feel . . . ," or "I value . . . ." It focuses on *oneself* or on the *relationship* (third self), not on the partner. It does not criticize or blame, but merely *states* a need or a value. When assertiveness calls for action, people may act affirmatively and constructively. To act critically, blamingly, or destructively is not assertiveness.

Recall at least three times recently in an intimacy relationship when you needed to be assertive, either for your own needs or values or for those of the third self. In each situation, did you act assertively, or not? Explain.

Recall times when you've invited an intimate partner to be assertive about himself or herself. Were they able to be?

"If it weren't for you, we wouldn't be in this mess."

"I feel as badly as you do. Let's clean things up."

"I see a problem that needs time and hard work. Can I help?"

Blaming is one of the commonest ways of blocking inner-core energies, for blaming implies that the blamer is somehow outside of and above the situation and, moreover, is able to see clearly the causes and reasons why things happen. Blaming flips an intimate relationship back into a game-playing one. It says, "You're not OK."

As an energizing alternative to blaming, try describing what you see, and *emphasize what needs to be done.* For example, instead of saying, "Why did you burn that expensive pot roast?" try, "I see you're disappointed at the burned roast. So am I. Let's think of something that will cheer up both of us."

In this way, with the focus placed on the third self (and not on the "one who's to blame") the creative energies of both partners can be mobilized and shared. Emphasizing what needs to be done together reaffirms the "I'm OK — You're OK" position of the relationship.

Are there moments in your life when intimacy tends to be destroyed by blaming? If so, give an example. Then, try formulating an alternative response that describes what you see and feel and emphasizes what needs to be done to preserve (or restore) intimacy.

Blaming response	*I'm OK — You're OK alternative*
______________________	______________________
______________________	______________________
______________________	______________________

"We made it through thick and thin together."

"We have shared many moments listening to beautiful music."

"We managed to raise a loving family."

Creating a third self and fostering its growth can be one of the most meaningful things in human life. For many, such third-self relationships are as valuable as life itself, for they mark the fulfillment of one's relating self. In them, life is not only experienced, it is *shared*.

Each intimate relationship is a source of new meanings: not merely in achieving a task, experiencing values, and coping with unavoidable suffering, but now in *achieving a task together*, in *experiencing shared values*, and in *coping together with unavoidable suffering.*

Each intimate relationship enriches your life in incalculable ways, and brings the entire human race one link closer to complete unity.

Consider your intimate relationships one at a time, and show how each has been a source of meaning in:

Achieving a task together

Experiencing shared values

Coping together with unavoidable suffering

Energy of the new self

Intimacy opens the new self to a new world of possibilities. It evokes the fullest potential of your *new individual self* in its ego states and inner core. It sets free the capacities of your *new relating self* in its many forms of transactions. And it allows for the birth of a *third self,* which can only happen when inner-core energies of two (or more) relating selves meet intimately in the dimension of betweenness.

Your *individual self* contains your unique ego states, which are meant to be energized and brought to their fullest capacities by the energy generated in your inner core. Inner-core energies include the *urge to be free* and create new life patterns, the *urge to experience* and explore your inner and outer worlds, and the *urge to make decisions* and activate them in meaningful ways.

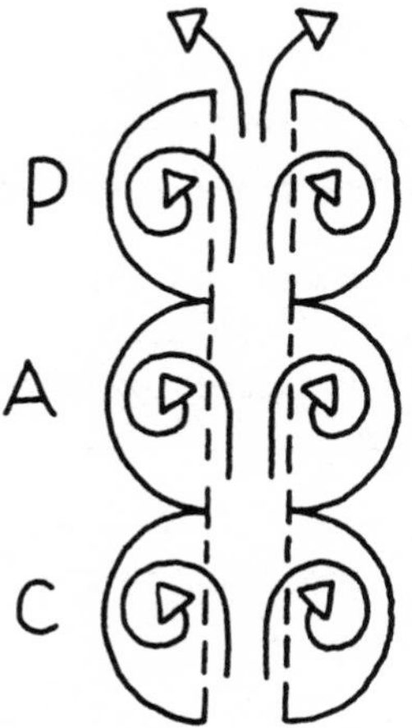

Ego states in the individual self being energized by inner core energy

In your *relating self,* other inner-core energies are meant to be released — for example, the urges to relate, to be intimate, to cooperate, to become involved and committed to social concern. These urges can energize your transactions into healthy interpersonal relationships and outward to areas of social need. Thus, inner-core energies may flow between you and each person with whom you relate, creating relationships that can not only mutually share energies, but can also spread and radiate these energies to others. When such a relationship operates on all ego state levels, as well as between inner cores, it might be diagrammed in the following way:

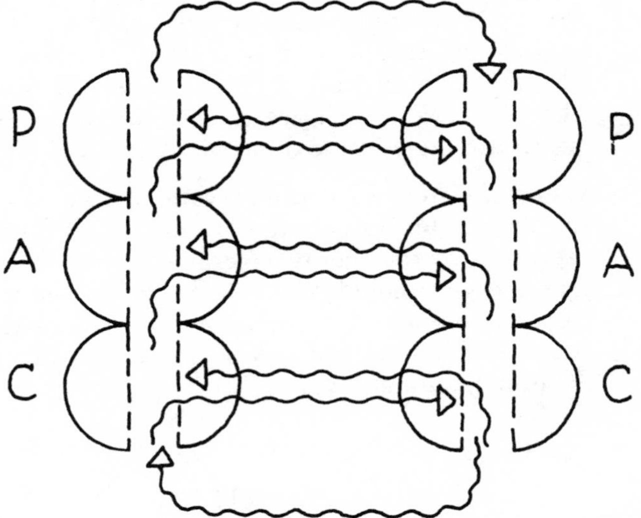

Inner core energies between relating selves

When the inner-core energies of two (or more) relating selves are shared, a deeper intimacy leading to the creation of a *third self* may result. This energized dimension of betweenness might be diagrammed as follows:

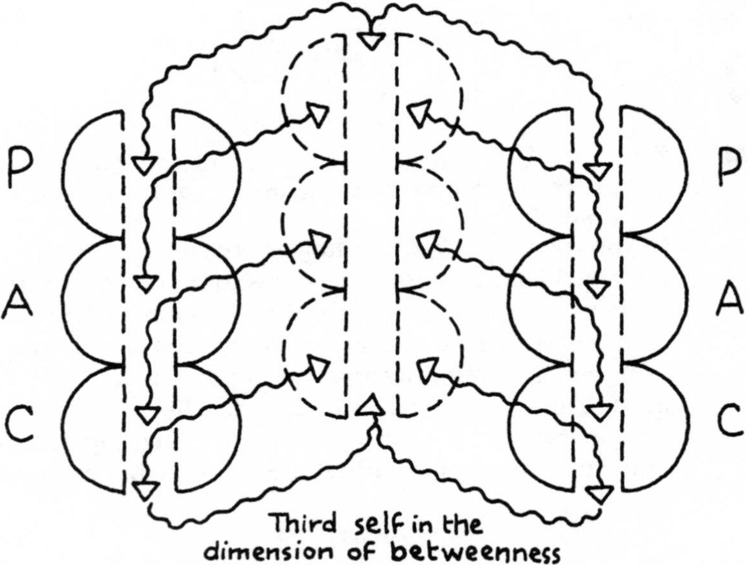

Third self in the dimension of betweenness

Third-self sharing, perhaps the most complete form of sharing, involves not only *self-awareness* (of the individual self) and *other-awareness* (of the relating self), but *together-awareness* (of the third self).

In a third self, not only are your ego state experiences shared, but your inner-core energies, and values and meanings are shared as well. When as a third-self intimate you are asked if you have a *why* to live for, you may reply on all three levels of a new self: your *individual self* may specify the whys it lives for, since it is unique and valuable in itself; your *relating self* may have other whys to live for, since it is capable of interacting and interrelating with others to create personal networks of love, learning, growth, and social concern in many forms; and, finally, your *third self* may have still other whys to live for that are discovered in the depths of intimacy, *shared whys* that may be explored only in the dimension of betweenness.

Cherish your New Self!

References

Chapter 1

[1]Muriel James and Dorothy Jongeward, *Born to Win* (Reading, Mass.: Addison-Wesley, 1971), p. 263.
[2]Viktor Frankl, *The Doctor and the Soul* (New York: Knopf, 1957), xii.

Chapter 2

[1]Muriel James and Dorothy Jongeward, *Born to Win* (Reading, Mass.: Addison-Wesley, 1971).
[2]From Muriel James, *Born to Love* (Reading, Mass.: Addison-Wesley, 1973), p. 198.
[3]Eric Berne, *What Do You Say After You Say Hello?* (New York: Grove Press, 1972, Bantam ed.), pp. 276–277. Emphasis added.
[4]Ibid., p. 249.
[5]Muriel James and Dorothy Jongeward, *The People Book* (Reading, Mass.: Addison-Wesley, 1975), p. 49.
[6]Muriel James, *Transactional Analysis for Moms & Dads* (Reading, Mass.: Addison-Wesley, 1974), p. 70.

Chapter 3

[1]Stephen B. Karpman, "Fairy Tales and Script Drama Analysis," *Transactional Analysis Bulletin* VII, no. 26 (April 1968): 39–43.
[2]See Muriel James and Dorothy Jongeward, *Born to Win* (Reading, Mass.: Addison-Wesley, 1971), p. 87

Chapter 4

[1]Muriel James and Dorothy Jongeward, *The People Book* (Reading, Mass.: Addison-Wesley, 1975), p. 160.
[2]Ibid., p. 147.

Chapter 6

[1]See Wilson Van Dusen, "The Natural Depth in Man," in Carl Rogers and Barry Stevens, *Person to Person: The Problem of Being Human* (Walnut Creek, California: Real People Press, 1967), p. 230.

Chapter 7

[1]Muriel James, "Self Reparenting: Theory and Process," *Transactional Analysis Journal* 4:3, July 1974.
[2]Eric Berne, *Principles of Group Treatment* (New York: Oxford University Press, 1964), p. 312.

[3]Ibid., p. 105. See also Eric Berne, *Transactional Analysis in Psychotherapy* (New York: Grove Press, 1961), pp. 233–234.
[4]Eric Berne, *Transactional Analysis in Psychotherapy* (New York: Grove Press, 1961), p. 60.

Chapter 9

[1]See Muriel James, *Born to Love* (Reading, Mass.: Addison-Wesley, 1973), pp. 140–146.
[2]Robert Goulding, "New Directions in Transactional Analysis: Creating an Environment for Redecision and Change," *Progress in Group and Family Therapy*, ed. by Clifford Sager and Helen Kapean (New York: Brunner/Mazel, 1972), p. 107. Also see Muriel James, *Techniques in Transactional Analysis for Psychotherapists and Counselors* (Reading, Mass.: Addison-Wesley, 1976), p. 2.
[3]Tabi Kahler and Hedges Capers, "The Miniscript," *Transactional Analysis Journal* (Jan. 1974), p. 28. See also Muriel James, *Techniques in TA*, op cit.

Chapter 10

[1]Eric Berne, *What Do You Say After You Say Hello?* (New York: Grove Press, 1972), Bantam ed., p. 31.

Chapter 11

[1]Virginia Satir, *Peoplemaking* (Palo Alto, Ca.: Science Behavior Books, 1972), p. 30.

Chapter 12

[1]Claude Steiner, "A Fairy Tale," *Transactional Analysis Bulletin* 9, no. 36 (1970): 146–149.
[2]Eric Berne, *Games People Play* (New York: Grove Press, 1964).
[3]Muriel James, *The OK Boss* (Reading, Mass.: Addison-Wesley, 1976).

Chapter 13

[1]Eric Berne, *Games People Play* (New York: Grove Press, 1964), p. 171.
[2]Muriel James and Dorothy Jongeward, *Born to Win* (Reading, Mass.: Addison-Wesley, 1971).
[3]Eric Berne, *What Do You Say After You Say Hello?* (New York: Grove Press, 1972), p. 23. See also Muriel James and Dorothy Jongeward, *The People Book* (Reading, Mass.: Addison-Wesley, 1975), p. 133–134.

[4]John James, "The Game Plan," *Transactional Analysis Journal* 3, no. 4 (October 1973), pp. 14–17.

[5]Robert Zechnick, "Good Games," *Transactional Analysis Journal,* January 1973, pp. 52–56. See also Eric Berne, *Games People Play* (New York: Grove Press, 1964).

[6]John James, "Positive Payoffs after Games," *Transactional Analysis Journal,* July 1976.

Chapter 14

[1]Muriel James, *Born to Love* (Reading, Mass.: Addison-Wesley, 1973), p. 75. See also Eric Berne, *Games People Play* (New York: Grove Press, 1964), p. 30.

[2]Thomas Gordon, *Parent Effectiveness Training* (New York: Wyden, 1970).

[3]See Muriel James and Louis M. Savary, *The Heart of Friendship* (New York: Harper & Row, 1976), pp. 89–90.

[4]See L. M. Savary, M. S. Paolini, and G. A. Lane, *Interpersonal Communication* (Chicago: Loyola University Press, 1975), p. 182.

Chapter 15

[1]Eric Berne, *Games People Play* (New York: Grove Press, 1964), p. 29. See also Muriel James and Dorothy Jongeward, *Born to Win* (Reading, Mass.: Addison-Wesley, 1971), p. 24.

Chapter 16

[1]Muriel James, *Born to Love* (Reading, Mass.: Addison-Wesley, 1972), p. 170.

[2]Eric Berne, *Games People Play* (New York: Grove Press, 1964), p. 17.

[3]See Alan Lakein, *How to Get Control of Your Time and Your Life* (New York: Wyden, 1973).

[4]Eric Berne, *What Do You Say after You Say Hello?* (New York: Grove Press, 1972), p. 25.

Chapter 17

[1]Muriel James and Louis M. Savary, *The Heart of Friendship* (New York: Harper & Row, 1976). See especially Chapter 2, "The Third Self of Friendship," pp. 14–32.

[4]Eric Berne, *What Do You Say After You Say Hello?* (New York: Grove Press, 1972), p. 25.

Index to Exercises